DANCE INTO BUSINESS

DANCE INTO BUSINESS

A how-to guide for dance students,
teachers and professionals

Richard Thom

Dance into Business
This edition 2018
Published by Independent Publishing Network
Typeset by Fakenham Prepress Solutions, Fakenham, Norfolk NR21 8NL

ISBN 978-1-78926-542-2 (Print)
ISBN 978-1-78926-543-9 (E-book)

CONTENTS

TABLES

ABOUT THE AUTHOR

Richard Thom grew up in Kuwait in the 1950s and 60s but was educated in Scotland. He is a Chartered Accountant with an honours degree in Business and Administration, majoring in Finance from the University of Portsmouth and a Diploma in Charity Accounting (DChA). He is a Fellow of both the Institute of Chartered Accountants in England and Wales (FCA) and the Royal Academy of Dance (FRAD).

From 1988 until 2015, Richard was the Director of Finance and Administration for the Royal Academy of Dance, an international Dance Awarding Organisation based in London and operating in over 60 countries. Prior to that he worked in audit (London), oil (Saudi Arabia), shipping (Japan), and automobiles (Guam).

Richard has been a speaker at national and international conferences, interviewed on US cable TV for *Spirit of Dance,* lectured to students on the Academy's dance degree programmes, delivered business seminars to teachers, written dance-related business briefings and articles for dance and business magazines and visited many of the countries where the Academy operates, meeting both teachers and students. He loves travelling and has visited more than 80 countries.

He wrote a booklet *"From Ballet to Business"* to accompany the lectures, and had published articles on *"Starting Your Own Business"* and *"Counting the Cost of Your Business"* in the Royal Academy of Dance's *Dance Gazette Supplement,* and *"Buying and Selling a School"* in the dance magazine *Dancing Times.* He also developed and wrote a series of business *Briefings* published by the Royal Academy of Dance as a member benefit.

This publication was born out of his interaction with dance professionals, teachers and graduates during that time.

He has participated in many committees, undertaken voluntary positions in employee associations, served on community associations in various roles, and undertaken dance consultancy and trouble-shooting assignments, nationally and internationally. He was a former Chairman of the Registration Board of the Council for Dance Education and Training CDET (now Council for Dance Drama and Musical Theatre CDMT), a Director of Youth Dance England (now part of One Dance UK), and is currently a Trustee of the Dancers Pension Scheme.

ACKNOWLEDGEMENTS

My thanks to Steve Andrews FCA and Judd Bankert CPA for their technical assistance; Karen Jennings for her time and constructive comments in the development of this book; Dr Dabney Bankert, Professor of English at James Madison University, VA for her academic and literary advice; Dr Susan Cooper and Dr Scilla Dyke MBE for their academic and professional input; Lynne Reucroft Croome LRAD PGCE BA (Hons) and Imogen Knight BA, Dip.RAD, Dip.TD (NBS), ARAD, AISTD for their experience as dance school owners and Registered teachers; Beatriz San Martin for her legal eye; Julie Bowers as an artistic development manager and former professional dancer; and to Steven for his patience and understanding.

PERMISSIONS

The author is grateful to Royal Academy of Dance for permitting the use of *Factsheet Nos 01, 04, 08* and *10*; *Terms of Engagement for Self-Employed Teachers* and *From Ballet to Business*. Penny Dain for permitting the use of *Spread the Word About Your School*.

☀ Courtesy of http://cliparting.com/free-light-bulb-clip-art-12531

INTRODUCTION

Dance into Business is intended primarily as a guide for dance students, teachers and professionals practising in a variety of contexts:

- Contemplating a change in career
- Taking up their first teaching post
- Planning their own business
- Setting up a freelance career
- Transitioning from employment to self-employment
- Returning to the work place
- Expanding or selling an existing business

The principles contained herein can be used by others seeking similar guidance.

This book was born out of a seminar first delivered by the author in 1991 to dance teachers as members of the Royal Academy of Dance, a global Dance Awarding Organisation. The seminar was delivered to fill a perceived gap in the attendees' knowledge base. Their expertise was teaching dance, learnt through experience or by graduating from dance teaching programmes that had concentrated on the practice and theory of dance, with little or no study of business. These teachers had successfully established dance schools and had acquired their business acumen through a combination of trial and error, shared experience and external learning.

The initial seminar was extended to workshops held around the United Kingdom and internationally, attracting teachers, dance school owners, transitioning dance professionals and young dance teachers starting out.

Among the success stories at the workshops, stories emerged of schools charging unrealistically low fees because their nearest competitors were not running their schools as businesses. Other teachers had been discouraged from opening schools in areas with existing schools due to an "unwritten rule" about competing with existing schools. Older teachers, on retirement, had simply closed or given away their business without realising the monetary value of their name, reputation, goodwill and profitability.

These dance teachers, whose lives had been dedicated to their profession and art form, had been unknowingly or unintentionally engaging in possible anti-commercial, anti-competitive and anti-profitable activity as well as walking away from a potential retirement provision. Their dance teacher education had derived from excellent dance teacher training courses whose training had concentrated on the practical delivery of teaching rather than including any content on the management and administration. Most small business owners today would agree that they spend much more time than they ever realised on the management of a business.

Teachers and dance professionals began approaching the author for individual practical business tips. A booklet *"From Ballet to Business"*[1] was written to accompany the lectures and subsequently provided to new teaching members of the Royal Academy of Dance.

Selected business articles were published in the Royal Academy of Dance's *Dance Gazette Supplement*[2][3] and the dance magazine *Dancing Times*[4] and these formed the basis for a series of business *Briefings* developed and written by the author and published by the Royal Academy of Dance. A number of these have been used as reference material in this publication.

Changes in dance teaching education and the promotion of continuing professional development have improved the business knowledge of dance teachers. Graduate, university validated and accredited dance teacher training courses and programmes now include business and career development within their course content. Organisations, course providers and mentoring programmes globally assist dance professionals to transition to new careers or to return to work.

Dance professionals encourage, guide, inspire, nurture and educate individuals and groups of all ages and abilities in different forms of dance, whether performing, coaching, mentoring, notating, choreographing, or teaching. They can provide personal coaching and mentoring to individuals already in the performing arts, to individuals keen to pursue a career in the performing arts as professional dancers, choreographers, producers, administrators and teachers; and teach group classes to students interested in dance as a leisure activity.

[1]   (Thom, From Ballet to Business, 1992–2014)
[2]   (Thom, Counting the Cost of Your Business, 1991)
[3]   (Thom, Starting Your Own Business, 1991)
[4]   (Thom, Buying and Selling a School, 1998)

It has been said that a good dancer does not always make a good teacher, just as a good teacher does not always make a good dancer. While "good" can be subjective, this comment can typically relate to the empathy, support, motivation and respect shown by a dancer and their partner or a teacher and their students, but it can apply equally to success in business. A teaching qualification or background does not necessarily provide all of the key components to a successful entrepreneurial life in dance. Using or turning dance ability into a business does not necessarily come easy, but the advantage is that the technical skills are there. The individual makes a business idea work. The individual is the business.

Questions to consider include deciding what you want to do with your skills? Whom do you want to work for, yourself or for someone else, or a combination of the two? Are you ready to be your own boss? Do you have the necessary resources and self-determination to succeed? Is there a market? How do you stay creative, be inspired and inspiring in your chosen art form, while at the same time leveraging and honing your skills to run a successful business? Where do you want to work or establish your own business, in your home country or overseas?

A dance business is not unique or original, but it is a market in which you can exploit your skills and qualifications. It maybe more sensible to choose a niche market that you are familiar with than trying to introduce something new.

If you are a *newly graduated* or *about-to-graduate* dance-teaching student, you might typically want to:

- Continue your studies at postgraduate or masters level, but use your teaching qualification to supplement your studies with casual part-time, term-time, or seasonal work; Or
- Gain more teaching experience in full-time employment; Or
- Work at a number of different dance schools and institutions, developing a portfolio of freelance work that may involve performing, management, choreography as well as teaching.

Dance schools and institutions are often in search of new teaching staff, particularly at the beginning of a new season, academic or school year. Northern hemisphere businesses will have a different season, academic or school year to those in the southern hemisphere; Or

- Take on some freelance work, but supplementing this with employment, offering job and financial security.

Dance schools operate mostly in the afternoons, evenings and weekends, so it would be possible to freelance as a dance teacher, while at the same time teaching or working for another dance or non-dance business; Or

● Go for it and set up a business with premises.

Occasionally, a student may have the opportunity to join a family dance business, or join or take over the management of their dance teacher's school with the prospect of buying it.

You need to consider which option might suit you best. Adopt a realistic approach to assist with your decision making. Consider a cautious approach, choosing between being employed by someone else and learning from them; or being employed initially, moving towards self-employment over time; or being employed and self-employed at the same time. Alternatively, take a more entrepreneurial approach, establishing your own business.

You might however *already be in the dance profession*, but want to:

● Transition from dancing professionally to freelancing or set up a business; Or

● Move from employment to freelancing or set up a business; Or

● Expand your existing dance business (or possibly to sell); Or

● Return to employment or start a business after a career break (raising a family, illness, looking after parents, etc.); Or

● Simply refresh your knowledge.

As with the newly graduated or about-to-graduate dance-teaching student, you need to be familiar with employment contracts and understand the terms as an employee; as a self-employed person, you need to understand the fundamentals of setting up, establishing and running a business.

Your business, as a freelancer, could be in a variety of contexts, with a mixed portfolio of work, teaching at multiple locations, or establishing a business. Being self-employed is a full-time job but you should not neglect your family, your relationships and your health. Thoughts and ideas should be channelled to optimise energy and enthusiasm. You need to find a niche to exploit and a good work/life balance to maintain.

This publication looks at demystifying some of the concepts around employment and self-employment. It looks at different types of employment and the main stages of getting into business: preparation, planning, setting up and starting out. It explains the principles of business plans, budgets, costing, pricing, cash flow, break-even, finance, operations, and other issues that can be key components to a successful business. It uses a dance school as the business model and contains hints and tips, some of which are generic, others specific to a dance school. The principles however can be applied to other dance businesses such as productions, conferences, workshops and course provision.

If you *already operate an existing school* and want to restructure or expand, you should already be familiar with many aspects of being in business. Expansion can bring its own challenges, but you can use the same tools as a start-up to determine whether you can afford it, whether there is a market, what additional funding resources are required and how you might obtain them.

As with those starting out or transitioning, you may decide to be cautious and take a phased approach to expansion over time, or decide to be more entrepreneurial and consider buying an existing school, merging with another, acquiring new or renting additional premises.

If you fall into any of these categories, this book is intended for you. Recognising your strengths and weaknesses and exploiting your dance experience can lead to success. If you are passionate about dance, teaching, hard work, are driven to succeed, motivated, resilient, committed and disciplined, this book is for you.

If you decide to take up employment or offer yourself as a freelancer to other businesses, you may wish to read those chapters that will assist in your decision. If you are starting out in business or contemplating a change in career, you may wish to read this book from the beginning to the end. If you are restructuring or expanding, you may choose to read relevant chapters. Some of the initial chapters may refer to ideas explored in more detail later in the book. The Contents page lists the major sub-headings within each chapter; and each chapter starts with a list of Key Points and an Introduction paragraph.

Using insight from working in the dance world, this publication contains helpful tips, practical examples and lists of points to consider. The author assumes readers could be living and working anywhere in the world and therefore the book has not been written to answer specific queries relating to individual cases or jurisdictions, as many different issues and laws will apply. It is intended only as a guide, and general hints and tips are marked by �

-☼-.

Whatever you decide, the author hopes this book guides you towards a successful business.

CHAPTER 1

CHOOSING YOUR OPTIONS

KEY POINTS

Employment status   Employment rights   Employee   Employment contracts
Non-resident foreign employment contracts   Worker   Zero hours contracts   Self-employed
Test of employment and self-employment   Advantages and disadvantages of employment
and self-employment   Employing staff or contracting freelancers   Portfolio careers
Entrepreneurship

This chapter examines employment and self-employment; the differences; the advantages and disadvantages and what you might or can expect.

Because of the complexity of the law, this chapter can only ever be a guideline. Employment and self-employment law differs in each country and some rights, benefits and flexibility are greater or less than others. Both can be subject to change as company law and tax legislation is introduced and amended. The "sharing economy" pioneered by Uber, Deliveroo and Airbnb and other technology companies is opening up opportunities for self-employment, but has prompted governments in the major economies to look at zero hours contracts, minimum wages and the relationship of tech companies providing "software platforms" and the changing nature of self-employment.

Self-employment is more suitable for individuals who are independent and want to offer their services as a freelancer to a number of businesses and institutions, or have a more entrepreneurial streak and want to set up their own business.

Employment, on the other hand, can be suitable for individuals wishing to supplement studies with part-time, term-time, or seasonal work; simply wishing to gain more experience in a paid position; or returning to the work force after a career break.

There is of course a halfway house where financial security or job stability offered by a combination or portfolio of paid employment and self-employment might be more attractive.

Employment status

There are generally three main types of employment status:

- Employee
- Worker
- Self-employed

An individual's employment status will define their employment rights and may or will influence an individual's decision. You will be the only person to decide which options will suit you best and when. You are the person who decides whether you are fit to start your own business. This puts a heavy responsibility on your shoulders as not everyone is suited to being self-employed, but an advantage is that many of your colleagues will be in the same industry and might be able to help in your journey.

Employment rights

An individual's employment rights will depend on whether they are an employee, worker or self-employed.

All employees are workers but not all workers are (classified as) employees. Consequently, an employee can have extra employment rights and responsibilities that do not apply to workers who are not considered employees in law. Generally, if a worker has a right, it will also apply to an employee, but not always vice versa.

These extra rights can include all, some, or none of the rights listed below depending on the country and its employment laws. The right to:

- ✓ Written statement of employment
- ✓ National minimum wage
- ✓ Holiday pay
- ✓ Paid maternity absence, paternity absence, adoption and shared parental absence
- ✓ Flexible working
- ✓ Sick pay or health care plans
- ✓ Pension or retirement plans
- ✓ Minimum notice period
- ✓ Protection against unfair dismissal
- ✓ Time off for emergencies
- ✓ Redundancy pay

✓ Maximum hours in a working day

✓ Maximum days in a working week

In order to qualify for some of these rights, an employee may be required to serve a minimum length of continuous employment. An employment contract should state how long the qualification or continuous employment period is.

An employment contract should specify the country of jurisdiction to provide the basis on which any disputes are settled.

Employee

At the beginning of a career, it can be often more beneficial to gain experience with the safety of guaranteed hours and remuneration. Becoming an employee can provide this security. An employee works to the terms and conditions within a contract *of* employment and is required to provide specific duties, as outlined in a job description.

Employment is a relationship between two parties – employer and employee – usually based on an employment contract:

- An **employer** hires the services of another (you) in accordance with the pay, terms and conditions documented in an employment contract.

- An **employee** (you) is a person hired to provide services to a business on a regular basis in exchange for a salary package and who does not provide these services as an independent business.

Contracts do not have to be written to be valid providing you have agreed the terms, but a written contract gives certainty. An offer letter, employment contract, job description and person specification should cover all aspects of your employment. These should be read together, as if a single contract:

- The elements of a contract are an **offer** (by the employer) and **acceptance** (by you, the employee).

- An **employment contract** defines the requirements of the job and stipulates the terms and conditions of employment. The employment contract is an agreement entered into voluntarily by both parties, creating a legal obligation between both parties.

- A **job description** provides a broad outline of your particular role, including job title, duties, scope, responsibilities etc.

- A **person specification** states the type of person that might fill the job, evidencing the skills, education and attributes required, which can accompany the advertisement of a job, and which might form part of the employment contract.

Additional information about the company culture, policies and procedures should be contained in an **employee handbook**, which usually forms part of an employee induction process. An employee handbook should provide clear guidance to employees, including procedures on dealing with disciplinary and grievance matters. Handbooks can be non-contractual because of the difficulty in keeping such books up-to-date, but provide an environment where issues can be dealt with fairly and consistently.

You are an employee if most of the following statements are true. You:

- ✓ Work regularly, apart from being on holiday, sick leave, or maternity/paternity absence
- ✓ Work a minimum number of hours and expect to be paid for the time worked
- ✓ Report or are accountable to an owner, director, manager or supervisor regarding your duties, including start and finish times
- ✓ Cannot substitute someone else to do your work
- ✓ Have tax and other statutory contributions automatically deducted from your wages (as appropriate to the particular jurisdiction)
- ✓ Receive paid holidays
- ✓ Are entitled to statutory employment rights and benefits (as appropriate to the particular jurisdiction)
- ✓ Can join (or opt out, if permitted) of a business's pension scheme (as appropriate to the particular jurisdiction)
- ✓ Work at the business's usual premises or elsewhere, if requested
- ✓ Are equipped (by the business) with the necessary materials and tools to undertake your work

Employment contracts

The content of employment contracts can differ from country to country. Some countries have mandatory clauses, determined by specific legislation. A comprehensive contract of employment allows an employer to specify an employee's duties and responsibilities – so you know what is expected of you. If you do not understand any of the terms in the employment contract, you should seek legal advice before signing any employment contract. If you feel that clauses need to be added or language clarified, do not be afraid to ask.

The following points should be included or covered, as a minimum, in a contract, employee handbook, accompanying job description and offer letter:

○ Names and details of both parties

○ Status as employee

- In some cases, employees, who may have freelance status for other work, may be wrongly considered by employers as *self-employed* – thus creating a situation where neither party is paying taxes. This situation has often arisen through historical practice rather than intent.

○ Start date

○ An end date, if a fixed term contract

○ Job title and job description setting out the employer's expectations

- A clause should explain how future changes to an employee's duties and responsibilities would be handled.

○ Place or places of work

- Some dance employers can have multiple locations, "branches" or places of work. If there is a clause requiring you to work at different locations, ensure there is an additional clause relating to the reimbursement of travel expenses between one location, "branch" and another (refer to Reimbursement of business expenses below).

○ Regular hours of work

○ Additional working hours

- Establish which working hours and or activities are included in your salary and which are paid in addition.

- You can be involved in performing, teaching, lecturing, end-of-term shows or graduations, summer schools and other activities, as well as planning and preparation. You could be asked to undertake distance-learning tutoring if you are in an academic environment. These additional hours can affect your workload. In some countries there are regulations relating to the maximum number of working hours.

○ Probationary period

- Trial, or probationary, periods with the option of a short notice period at the end of the trial can safeguard both parties if the employment does not work out. It can assist in an earlier, or less stressed, departure.

- Probationary periods may relate to academic terms or performance seasons rather than single months, so that both parties have the security of a term's teaching or a season's performance.

○ Assessments or reviews

- Assessments or reviews enable both parties (employee and employer) to discuss the working relationship on a regular basis. The first work assessment or review might be at the conclusion of the probationary period. Regular assessments or reviews thereafter might be every 12 months.

○ Gross salary
○ Salary deductions
○ Method and frequency of salary payment

- A clause should state gross salary before tax and deductions.

- A clause should state the rate at which additional work is paid.

- Salary deductions may be both statutory and non-statutory. Statutory deductions may differ from country to country but can include taxation, social insurance and any other similar types of deductions. Non-statutory deductions are those agreed with an employer. All of the circumstances in which the employer can make deductions from the employee's salary should be documented in order to avoid misunderstanding, disagreement, or dispute.

○ Reimbursement of business expenses

- A clause should state what business expenses can be reimbursed.

- You might need to buy props, small equipment and material to conduct classes; pay for travel or petrol between different business locations; or pay for goods that the employer should normally pay for.

- If an employer does not reimburse you for business expenses incurred in the course of employment, you should determine whether you could claim these as an allowable employment expense under your tax code.

- An employer may have multiple locations, "branches" or places of work. It is possible that some of these will be in another country. You should establish what allowances are provided or costs reimbursed when visiting other branches or offices.

If your employer is in education, you may be required to undertake distance-learning tutoring. You should establish what costs are reimbursed for the distance-learning tutoring.

○ Paid holidays per year

○ Statutory holidays per year

○ Working on holidays

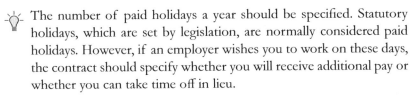 The number of paid holidays a year should be specified. Statutory holidays, which are set by legislation, are normally considered paid holidays. However, if an employer wishes you to work on these days, the contract should specify whether you will receive additional pay or whether you can take time off in lieu.

○ Restrictions on holiday times

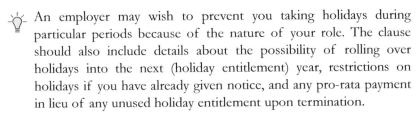 An employer may wish to prevent you taking holidays during particular periods because of the nature of your role. The clause should also include details about the possibility of rolling over holidays into the next (holiday entitlement) year, restrictions on holidays if you have already given notice, and any pro-rata payment in lieu of any unused holiday entitlement upon termination.

An employer might schedule activities at Christmas and other cultural and religious festive periods, during holidays or outside term time such as end-of-term shows and summer school or workshops.

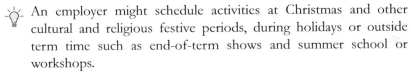 You may also be restricted if you have been contracted to undertake distance learning tutoring in an academic year that differs from the main contract year.

○ A sickness and disability clause should state whom you have to inform when you are sick, when you must inform that party, and what happens to your salary in the event of short, medium or long-term absences.

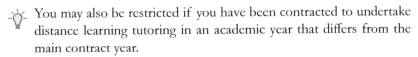 Employees, unlike self-employed individuals, are not normally required to find a replacement unless specified in the job description. Some countries have statutory minimum sickness payments; some businesses have their own sickness policies, which exceed statutory minimums.

○ A pension clause should state whether your employment comes with or without a pension provision. Some countries have statutory pension schemes.

- ☀ Consider whether you wish to join or opt out of the employer's scheme (if offered), or provide for your own scheme in the absence of one.

○ A notice clause should include the period of notice given either by the employer or by the employee following successful completion of the probationary period. Employees are usually protected by law from dismissal without notice or without going through the appropriate procedures, but an employer might be able to dismiss an employee without notice in certain circumstances. Reasons for dismissal of this type can vary from jurisdiction to jurisdiction, but it would be expected practice for an employer to spell out in a separate grievance and disciplinary policy what might constitute behaviour leading to an action of this type, often referred to as *dismissal for gross misconduct*.

○ A data protection or intellectual property clause can impose restrictions on the creation of or the use of data obtained while in employment. This is intended to protect confidential and commercial information belonging to the employer.

- ☀ This is particularly true where employees might have access to parent, carer and student personal details as a dance teacher in charge of class participant registers. An employee should not use data lists from a previous employer, as this will invariably result in a breach or misuse of data.

- ☀ Parents, carers and students can build up a significant loyalty to a teacher. A freelance teacher or prospective dance school owner needs to ensure that any decision by the parent, carer or student to follow the dance teacher is the parent, carer or student's decision and the parent, carer or student's decision alone.

○ The legal jurisdiction of the contract, *i.e.,* which country's law is used to interpret disputes arising from employment.

○ Some employers may have an additional clause such as a restrictive covenant clause, which can impose conditions on an employee when working for a future employer.

- ☀ These are known as non-compete or covenant-not-to-compete clauses, NCC and CNC respectively.

- ☀ A restrictive covenant can prevent an employee from competing for a set period and within a defined geographical area on leaving employment, as well as trying to prevent them from encouraging other employees to leave and work in a competing business.

Non-resident foreign employment contracts

Dance is a mobile profession. Dance professionals can be offered and accept a job in countries outside of their normal residency. In such cases, an employee should ensure that the terms offered are sufficient and affordable to live in the country where the job is located. You should satisfy yourself about:

✓ Cost of living in the country

✓ Cost of travel to take up the contract and who provides and pays for it

✓ Cost of accommodation and who provides and pays for it

✓ Taxation and any other types of statutory and non-statutory salary deductions

✓ Professional indemnity insurance and who provides and pays for it

In addition to the types of clauses for regular employment contracts, you should also consider the following points for any foreign employment contract or engagement:

○ Length of contract

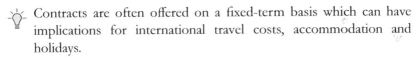 Contracts are often offered on a fixed-term basis which can have implications for international travel costs, accommodation and holidays.

○ Social insurance

If you have to pay into an overseas social insurance scheme, check what happens to any future entitlements and any action you may have to take to safeguard future entitlements when the contract ends and you leave the country.

You should also consider paying voluntary social insurance contributions (if possible) in your normal country of residence to safeguard any future government pension entitlements.

○ Travel to take up appointment

Some employers will only pay the cost of air travel at the beginning and end of the contract. If you want to return home mid-contract for a holiday it could be at your own expense. Also, establish who is responsible for the return airfare if you give notice before the end of the contract period.

○ Work visa

- Ensure that you are either eligible for work or your employer obtains a valid work visa for you. Also, ensure that you are able to retain your passport during the employment period.

○ Accommodation

- Some employers provide accommodation. It should be clear whether the cost is absorbed by the employer, provided through an additional allowance, or deducted from your salary. Determine what the cost covers, how far the accommodation is located from the place of work, and what type of accommodation is provided – house, apartment, dormitory, single, sharing. Also, establish who is responsible for your share of the accommodation cost if you give notice before the end of the contract period.

○ Holidays

- Determine if there are any restrictions on holidays. Some employers provide visas or issue contracts that do not allow you to leave the country during the term of the contract. In this case, holidays would have to be taken in-country.

- Paid holidays in your host country may be more or less than those in your normal country of residence.

○ Statutory holidays

- As an employee, do not expect cultural and religious festive holidays and statutory holidays to be the same as the country of your usual residence, or even on the same calendar dates.

○ The legal jurisdiction of the contract, *i.e.,* which country's law is used to interpret disputes arising from employment.

Make sure both you and the employer sign each other's copies and keep all documents in a safe place in case you need them. It is also good practice to keep copies of your payslips.

Worker

A worker will also work within a contract of employment and carry out the work personally. This type of work can be referred to as casual work, agency work, freelance work, seasonal work, or zero hours work.

Someone is likely to be a worker if most of these apply:

✓ They occasionally do work for a specific business

✓ They only work when they want to

✓ They had to agree with the business's terms and conditions to get work

✓ They are under the supervision or control of a manager or director

✓ They cannot substitute someone else to do their work

✓ The business makes statutory deductions on their pay

✓ The business provides their materials, tools or equipment

The rights of these types of work can be less than those of a regular employee due to the nature of the relationship with the employer.

There is usually no entitlement to:

✓ Minimum notice periods

✓ Protection against unfair dismissal

✓ Right to request flexible working

✓ Time off for emergencies

✓ Statutory redundancy pay

Zero hours contracts[1]

The changing character of work and consumption in the digital age, where people can work flexibly from anywhere and consumers can buy online, may have given self-employment and zero hours contracts a boost.

Zero hours contracts are also known as casual contracts. Zero hours contracts are usually for "piece work" or "on call" work, *e.g.,* interpreters, data processors, taxi drivers. This means:

○ Workers are "on call" to work when employers need them

○ Employers do not have to give workers work

○ Workers do not have to do work when asked

Zero hours workers in the United Kingdom are entitled to statutory annual leave and the national minimum or living wage in the same way as regular workers.

Employers cannot stop a zero hours worker from seeking work elsewhere. United Kingdom law states workers can ignore a clause in a zero hours contract if banned from:

[1] (HM Government, 2018)

○ Looking for work

○ Accepting work from another employer

Employers remain responsible for health and safety of workers on zero hours contracts.

This type of employment might be suitable for an individual who wants to fit in employment around full-time or continuing education or needs some work but not fixed in any formal way, and for an employer who might want to cover sickness or unexpected absences of employees or freelancers.

Self-employed

Self-employed persons can also be known as sole traders, sole proprietors, freelancers, freelance contractors, independent contractors, independent or contract workers. Appendix 1 lists the names used in various countries.

Self-employed persons run their own businesses and work:

● On their own (own-account workers).

● On their own but engaging employees or freelance contractors in the business.

● In a partnership of two or more.

● In a partnership of two or more but engaging employees or freelance contractors in the business.

In some countries, self-employed persons can hold jobs defined as "self-employment jobs" – that is, jobs where the pay is directly dependent upon the profits derived from the goods and services provided. However, in other countries there is a test of self-employment.

Self-employment differs from employment in a number of ways. These are examined below.

Test of employment and self-employment

A person can generally be considered as **self-employed** if work is derived from two or more sources; but in some cases, this distinction is not always clear-cut or followed. It can depend on the type of employer, work or affiliation. For example:

● A government body may be required to treat all workers as employees, irrespective of the number of days, hours worked or the status of the individual; Or

- An employer finds it easier to treat all workers as employed; Or
- The work, in all practicality, satisfies the employment attributes; Or
- The workplace is unionised, and the union requires the employer to regard all workers as employees.

Employment provides more benefits for the employee, but costs more to the employer, while self-employment provides independence to the worker but more risk.

There is a general test in the United Kingdom to determine whether someone is an employee or self-employed:

If the answer is **YES** to the following questions, you are probably an **employee**:

○ Do you have to do the work yourself, rather than hire someone else to do it?

○ Can someone tell you at any time what to do, when and how to do it?

○ Are you paid by the hour, week, or month?

○ Can you earn overtime pay?

○ Do you work set hours or a given number of hours per week/month?

○ Do you work at the premises of your employer, or at a place/places determined by them?

If the answer is **YES** to this different set of questions, it will generally mean you are **self-employed**:

○ Do you have a final say in how the business is run?

○ Do you risk your own money in the business?

○ Are you responsible for meeting losses as well as taking profits?

○ Do you provide the major items of equipment you need to do your job?

○ Are you free to hire other people of your own choice to do the work you have taken on?

○ Do you pay to correct unsatisfactory work in your own time and at your own expense?

While the above questions are not absolute, they can help in determining work status. Other countries have similar definitions, although they may be expressed differently – for example, in Portugal, the definition of self-employment is expressed as:

○ When carrying out work, the worker is able to choose the processes and means to use, as they will be totally or partially their own property.

○ The worker is not obliged to comply with a working time schedule or minimum work periods, unless this is due to the application of legal provisions governing employment.

○ The worker may sub-contract other individuals to substitute him/her when carrying out work.

○ The activity of the worker is not integrated in the structure of the production process, the work organisation or the company's hierarchy.

○ The worker's activity is a non-core element in the organisation and pursuit of the employer's objectives.[2]

There are some "grey areas" in the dance industry. Some employers rely on their employees to provide the equipment to do the job, *e.g.,* dance teachers often bring in their own CD players, MP3 players, IOS iPads and iPhones, Android tablets and phones or recorded music players, and their playlists. This may not be regarded as providing major items of equipment, but rather a means of using the skills of the employee and maintaining artistic input. An employer might also require the employee to hold appropriate music licences for classes, or provide a computer or laptop and phone at home, if employed to carry out distance-learning tutoring.

☀ Employees should ensure that they are either reimbursed for any costs or can include them within their own tax code as employment expenses. (Refer to *Chapter 11: Paying Taxes.*)

If you decide to run your own dance school or another type of business with employees, there is no doubt you are self-employed because you become the "employer". However, if you offer your services as self-employed in whatever capacity, then you will need to satisfy the test of self-employment.

As referred to above, in some jurisdictions, you must earn income from at least two different sources to be considered self-employed. In some jurisdictions, employers have become responsible for ensuring that the employee is eligible or has the right to work and that their employment status is correct within the law.

Advantages and disadvantages of employment and self-employment

In deciding whether to be employed or self-employed, the following advantages and disadvantages should be considered:

---

[2] (Cabrita, Perista, Rego & Naumann, 2009)

Employment – advantages

1 Security

Employment can provide financial security, job stability and job profile. You will receive a salary on a predetermined date (or dates) each month, taxes will be deducted automatically, and you will benefit from any employment rights, social and health insurance, pension or retirement plans. You will also receive paid holiday periods.

2 Teamwork

You will be part of a team, of different sizes, working together towards shared goals. Colleagues will support your work and management will support your actions. You will have resources to fall back on. In self-employment, you would have to find those resources or rely on yourself. Self-employment brings credit for success, but also the responsibility for any failures.

3 Commitment

Some employers can contribute to ongoing training or continuing professional development costs in exchange for a commitment from you.

Employment – disadvantages

1 Self-expression

Your artistic or creative ideas may not be curtailed in your role, but they can be "tempered" to meet the expectations of the employer. You might feel stifled because your aims do not always agree with your employer's vision. Owners will have the ultimate decision-making power, while you will not. Conversely, if you are self-employed you can operate as you want, and will have the ability to develop the business to match your personal vision.

2 Earning potential

The employer's pay structure dictates your salary as an employee.

3 Supervision

You will have to take orders from the owner. A person who dislikes authority and directives may see this as a disadvantage.

4 Flexibility

Your time is in the hands of your employer, which may make it more difficult to juggle individual circumstances.

Self-employment – advantages

1 Independence

You will have ownership and a sense of achievement in creating and operating your own business.

2 Vision

You will be able to impose your own vision and standards. You can offer a more personalised service with local knowledge, roots and ties with more appeal to potential customers in the local community.

3 Control

You can maintain artistic and policy control. You can set your location, schedule and hours, and decide when to work. For example, you could take a weekday off and possibly work one day on the weekend; or work longer hours three days a week and have the remaining four days off. An employee, although entitled in some jurisdictions to flexible hours, generally has to work within a business's core hours. In practical terms, however, some types of business have less scope for truly flexible hours because of the demands of the customer.

4 Enjoyment

Your skills and expertise are being used in an environment of your choice, and this should show through and inspire confidence in your customers.

5 Decision making

You can make decisions quickly and swiftly, providing for the needs of customers and the business. You can decide how you work and whom you work with.

6 Overhead costs

You can work from home or a location outside of your home. Travelling costs from your home, if it contains your office, to work locations can be treated (in some jurisdictions) as a business expense, whereas if working as an employee, travel-to-work costs would not be a business expense.

7 Money

You can control your income; the opportunity for growth is potentially limitless. If you need a temporary or permanent income increase, you can choose to work longer hours or find new clients to generate additional revenue. You retain the profits of the business. There is potential for earning more as a self-employed person than there is as an employee.

Self-employment – disadvantages

1 Taxes, insurance and licences

There are no automatic company benefits such as sick pay or health plans, pension, or retirement plans. The self-employed need to make provision for:

✓ Social insurance or health insurance

✓ Professional indemnity insurance

✓ Pension or retirement plans

✓ Tax on net earnings

✓ Music licences

✓ Continuing professional and business development

2 Marketing

In addition to dance aptitude, you will need to demonstrate entrepreneurial attributes including business, communication and people skills. A start-up business requires familiarity with not only blogs, webpages, texts, apps but also more traditional forms of marketing such as business cards, fliers and anything else that will attract attention to the business. Name recognition can be of great importance to someone who is self-employed – "presence" in the marketplace is paramount.

3 Commitment

While dance is a vocation and most dance professionals enjoy their work, self-employment does not suit everyone. Running a successful business requires dedication. It can be hard to separate business from work when operating a business from home. Some dance businesses, such as dance schools, operate primarily in the afternoons, evenings and weekends, which can be disruptive to family life. Without a good work/ life balance, self-employed people can run into working around the clock and on weekends, and may ultimately suffer burnout or mental health issues. Do not let your business take you over.

4 Liability

Being self-employed, you are entirely responsible for the success (and failure) of your business, and have to ensure the business earns money. Lack of motivation, discouragement, family commitments, or physical factors such as illness or injury can jeopardise this success and – crucially – your income.

Employing staff or contracting freelancers

All types of business can employ or contract staff, irrespective of the business structure you might choose. An employment contract is a Contract *of* Service while a self-employed agreement is a Contract *for* Services.

You should behave reasonably and responsibly as an employer and apply the same safeguards and benefits you might seek from employment to your own employees or freelancers. Professional advice should be sought when drawing up employment contracts for your own employees, and a Contract *for* Services for freelancers, ensuring that all the points you would want and expect for yourself have been covered.

Chapter 16: Engaging Freelancers looks at some terms of engagement that might be included in a Contract *for* Services. The content and substance of the clauses give general guidance regarding such engagement. You should also take advice on the rights and duties of an employer towards employees, workers and the self-employed.

If you employ a non-earning spouse or other family members, this employment should be paid at a commercial rate, related to the amount of work they do, and must be for work within the business. An actual transfer of funds must be made, *i.e.*, payments must be made.

Portfolio careers

Dance professionals have been practising for many years what is now called a portfolio career. Portfolio working can be defined as where an individual has more than one strand to their career. The private and public sectors offer many opportunities for a dance professional with the right qualifications, skills, attributes and time.

An employer or employers can engage you as an employee for part of a working week under a Contract *of* Service, and the remainder of the week you can provide services to other businesses on a self-employed basis under a Contract *for* Services. This type of arrangement works well when an employer requires an employee for a short period, or can only offer limited work. Alternatively, you can provide services to a number of businesses in exchange for a fee and those services will form part of a freelance business.

Dance professionals often use their specialism to mix and match their skills or their employment mix. Dancers can mix dancing, coaching and teaching; freelancers can teach at multiple schools; dance school owners can run their own school, teach class and undertake community work; or a part-time student can study, teach as a freelancer and be employed in a regular paid job.

 If you only work for one employer, you would be normally regarded as **employed** if this work is regular and forms a significant part of your working week.

The advantage of portfolio working is that it marries flexibility, variety and quality. The options can be endless but they do require you to be able to manage time and maintain a balance. You are your own business.

Entrepreneurship

In determining the direction of your career, you need to look at yourself. Do you have the personal attributes for starting a business? Is it in your blood? What makes you happy? Do you feel you have a calling, or does your family own a business or run an existing dance school? Do you like taking calculated risks and solving issues where people have let you down? Are you happy to work long hours? Does lack of money worry you?

Many of the questions that you might ask yourself might well come true. You can work long hours, become stressed, a "jack of all trades", money can become tight; you can take risks from time to time, and you will have to solve problems. On the other hand, you will feel motivated, a sense of achievement, and pride in your work.

Self-employment is not for everyone and at times can be overwhelming, but it can be incredibly rewarding. It is your character and skills that will need to carry you through and make a success.

CHAPTER 2

BECOMING SELF-EMPLOYED

KEY POINTS

Planning and research   Environmental factors   Branding and marketing   Setting goals and milestones   As a freelancer   As a business   Getting help

As discussed in Chapter 1, self-employed persons can work on their own as own-account workers or with a partner, or on their own or with a partner but engaging employees or freelance contractors.

Self-employment can range from offering services to a number of other businesses to starting your own business. There are a number of issues to consider, whether you are starting out as a freelancer offering your services to a number of businesses, or starting your own business.

This chapter considers those issues.

Planning and research

Your business idea starts with you. You should consider sharing it with others to help you reinforce it, improve it and to make it viable, treat it as a form of idea incubation. Identify a business mentor when you want to ask a question, and who can help you ask the questions you did not know to ask. Whom you use to test your idea and plans is up to you, but the more they are involved the more likely strengths and weaknesses, opportunities and threats can be identified, resulting in a more robust business idea. If you have already found potential partners and team members then they could be your sharing group.

You should demonstrate your leadership in the exercise, as it is your idea that you want to see developed and commercially presented. It will help turn an idea into a business.

You should understand as much as possible about your market so you can develop a successful business strategy. You need to collect sufficient information and data – about the market, your potential customers, your competitors, your product, and pricing – for your Business Plan and strategy to be realistic. This research can take two approaches – desk and field. The former involves researching through the internet, library or other static resources, and the latter talking to potential customers, competitors, suppliers, potential employees and other interested parties.

Sources of desk research can range from banks, government departments, local authorities and dance student theses, to newspapers, journals, social media and websites. Field research can range from being a "secret shopper", dropping leaflets to gauge interest and conducting surveys, to watching performances and visiting after-school clubs. It is also possible to buy data from companies where consent has been given or the information is legally available.

Environmental factors

You should consider a mixture of micro- and macroenvironmental factors.

The **microenvironment** refers to the internal environment of the business. This can include, for example, employees and freelancers interacting with each other and customers and suppliers; your handling of complaints; customer service; and outstanding fees. It involves an understanding of the type of consumer market you will operate in and who is buying or using your products and services and why. You should always keep an eye on your competitors and develop a strategic advantage over them. A further aspect of the microenvironment is how media articles, public opinion, government legislation, residents associations and the public might affect your particular business.

The **macroenvironment** refers to those factors that are part of larger society and influence the microenvironment. These can be expressed using a PESTEL analysis that involves the collection of political, economic, social (demography), technology, environmental and legal (culture) factors that may affect your business.

○ **P**olitics includes all laws, government agencies and groups that might place limitations on your business.

○ **E**conomy refers to the purchasing power of your potential customers and the ways in which people spend their money.

○ Demography (**S**ocial) looks at the size, density, location, age, gender, race and occupation of your immediate marketplace and helps with understanding the different characteristics of each segment and identifying your target market.

○ **T**echnology is the fastest-changing factor in the macroenvironment. This includes all types of development, from apps and software to payment systems and credit cards. It requires a business to update its technology to stay ahead.

○ The natural **E**nvironment normally affects all businesses, for example floods, fires, earthquakes, pandemics and other natural disasters that might stop customers buying or businesses existing.

○ The cultural (**L**egal) environment affects businesses because institutions, basic values and beliefs of a group of people can affect how your business behaves.

Branding and marketing

Branding and marketing are crucial factors in the success of your business.

Branding is the strategy – identity, message, experience and image that you want your customers to identify, remember and love. It presents your business – from the logo, trade mark, brand and strapline to classes, interaction with students, suppliers, volunteers, team and board – as a package.

The sort of questions you need to consider for a successful brand identity should include:

✓ Where do you see you or your business going? (Vision)

✓ What do you or your brand believe in and stand for? (Values)

✓ How do you or your brand differ from others? (Strengths)

✓ How do you want yourself or your brand to present itself? (Personality)

✓ What do you or your brand promise? (USPs)

✓ What do you want customers to associate with you or your brand? (Qualities)

✓ What do you want customers to say about you or your business? (Superlatives)

Marketing is the tactic – research, advertising, promotion and customer care. It sells your brand to the world. Once your brand identity has been established, plan how to get your message across through your marketing activities. For example:

✓ Aligning branding with marketing and business goals

✔ Positioning the business in relation to potential customers and competitors

✔ Creating marketing programmes and messages by target audience and class

✔ Identifying which type of media to focus on – mainstream media, direct mail, social media, viral video, inter alia

✔ Complying with advertising standards

✔ Deciding what messages and USPs to promote via which media

✔ Building relationships with customers

When branding and marketing work together, a freelancer can benefit from a good reputation and a higher chargeable rate, and a business can benefit from a loyal customer base, brand quality and awareness, potentially premium pricing and mind share or customer referral.

 Be aware of spending too much in the beginning. Expenditure should be scalable according to budget and need. The personal touch can be your most effective marketing tool.

Setting goals and milestones

Goals and milestones complement each other and provide a critical path. Goals define where you are going; milestones let you know if you are actually getting there.

Goals describe how you or your business will look in a year's time, or longer. They can act as a source of inspiration and a sense of objective.

A milestone comes in handy as a check and balance system when assessing achievement of the goal. Milestones are actions and achievements necessary to make progress toward goals.

Stick to goals and milestones you have set. This can be hard if you are operating on your own, but easier if you share and agree them with your future or current team, depending on whether you are starting, restructuring or expanding a business. By including team members in this process, they can develop a sense of ownership towards the goals, with a better chance of achievement. This can be reflected in their commitment towards achieving the milestones. Setting clear goals helps to avoid misunderstandings between employer, the team and stakeholders.

Goals

Create goals, which are SMART – specific, measurable, achievable, realistic and timely. When a goal is tangible, you have a better chance of making it specific, measurable, and thus achievable.

1 **Specific**

A specific goal has a greater chance of being accomplished than a general goal. To set a specific goal you should be able to answer these questions:

- Who or what is involved?
- What do I want to accomplish?
- Where is it located?
- When will I accomplish it?
- Which requirements or resources do I need?
- What constraints are holding me back?
- Why am I setting this goal?

2 **Measurable**

Establish criteria for measuring progress toward the attainment of each goal you set. If you can measure your progress, you will stay on track, reach your target dates and encourage yourself to reach the remaining goals. To determine if your goal is measurable, you should ask questions such as:

- How much?
- How many?
- How will I determine when it is accomplished?

3 **Achievable**

When identifying goals that are important to you, you need to find ways to make them happen. You need to develop the attitude, aptitude, ability, skill and financial capacity to stretch out and reach them.

4 **Realistic**

A goal must represent an objective, which you are willing and able to work towards. It can be both high and realistic, but ensure that every goal represents substantial progress.

5 **Timely**

A goal should be accomplished within a time frame. A time frame makes a goal more realistic.

Milestones

You might have set goals for different periods, for example weekly, monthly, quarterly, half-yearly, annually.

If you are starting a business, ensure your team knows the goals and what you expect of them. Examples of goals and milestones that might contribute to opening the business on time could be:

Table 2.1: Example of Goals and Milestones

		By end of
Business Plan	Complete research	1st month
Business structure	Complete research	1st month
Funding	Identify need and consider investors	2nd month
Advisers	Identify need and consider advisers	2nd month
Premises	Start search for suitable premises	2nd month
Business Plan	Complete first draft	1st quarter
Business structure	Initiate and set up appropriate structure	4th month
Branding	Register business name, trade mark, domain and social media name	4th month
Premises	Complete on lease/purchase/rental terms	4th month
Staff	Start recruitment process	5th month
Promotion	Design website and social media	2nd quarter/half year
Administration	Develop and write rules and regulations	2nd quarter/half year
Administration	Develop and write appropriate policies and procedures	2nd quarter/half year
Administration	Develop and write promotional handbook	2nd quarter/half year
Systems	Select appropriate database, accounting software, mobile apps and payment systems	7th month
Premises	Make spaces suitable for purpose	3rd quarter
Resources	Identify and purchase equipment	3rd quarter
Administration	Plan timetable	3rd quarter
Advertising	Devise and start media campaign	3rd quarter
Administration	Purchase appropriate insurance policies	10th month
Business	Ready to open	4th quarter

Most milestones generally have cost implications, so ensure the costs have been included in your Business Plan. Example of costs could be:

Table 2.2: Example of costs associated with Milestones

	Set up costs	Ongoing costs
Initiate and set up appropriate business structure	Initial legal costs	Annual registration
Explore and finalise lease/purchase/rental	Initial legal costs	Renewal costs
Make spaces suitable for purpose	Decoration	Maintenance costs
Staff recruitment process	Recruitment costs	Replacement costs
Register a business name, trade mark, domain and social media name	Initial legal costs, trade mark filing costs, domain name registration costs	Renewal or re-registration
Design website and social media	Initial design costs	Updates
Identify and purchase equipment	Resources	Maintenance costs
Select appropriate database, accounting, mobile apps and payment systems	Purchase, leasing or subscription	Periodic leasing or subscription payments
Set up accounting system	Bookkeeping fees	Bookkeeper
Purchase appropriate insurance policies	Initial premiums	Annual premiums
Plan timetable	Time and staff cost	Time and staff cost
Develop and write appropriate policies	Time and staff cost	Time and staff cost
Develop and write promotional handbook	Design and print	Updates
Devise and start social media/media campaign	Media consultants	Time and staff cost Advertising cost

Taking your planning, research, environmental factors, branding and marketing, consider the following.

As a freelancer

If you wish to set up your business as a freelancer offering your services to a number of businesses and institutions, there are fewer issues to consider than if you are setting up a business with premises and employing or contracting a team:

1   Your market

Dance, in all its forms, is a growing market. As well as its theatrical and artistic presentation, it covers a number of career and lifestyle choices, among them educational, community, recreational, keeping fit, dance and older people, dance and disability, cultural, young people, health and well-being.

Choose the market segment on which to base your freelance business – whether by career or lifestyle choices, benefits, dance genre(s) or any combination thereof.

 Choose how – as a teacher, mentor, coach, dancer, choreographer, educator, producer, administrator, critic, writer, photographer, or costumier – there are many options.

 Ensure your choice is achievable.

2 Your customers

You will need to identify those businesses that you can offer your services to.

 You could form a co-sharing relationship with another freelancer, helping them out when sick or taking on work when they have too many offers.

3 Your location

You may find that your home location is not convenient for travelling to the businesses that have contracted you.

 Freelancers can find themselves criss-crossing counties to contracts. You will have decide how best to manage this.

4 Your marketability

You will need to ensure that you have the skills and attributes that businesses and the market segment you have chosen want.

 Ensure you have the right skills. Acquire additional skills or upgrade your qualifications through continuing professional development (CPD).

 Keep up-to-date with your profession and any regulatory requirement when working with children or healthcare, such as Disclosure and Barring (DBS)[1] or country equivalent.

 Adhere to your professional body's Code of Conduct and Professional Practice.

 Identify any Unique Selling Propositions (USPs) to promote yourself.

---

[1] (HM Government, 2018)

5 Fees and hours

Calculate your personal needs. The fees you charge for your services should be realistic to provide you with sufficient income.

 Fees should be based upon the hours you intend to work and your overall income needs.

 You should be aware of what businesses are willing to pay for similar services, and what other freelancers are charging.

 Acceptable fees can differ according to the type of employer, institution, type and content of engagement, contract, industry, geographic region, urban or rural area.

 Revisit your overall needs if you have to accept a lower rate; determine what effect a lower income might have on your lifestyle and personal needs and how you can resolve it.

6 Your terms of engagement

Chapter 16: Engaging Freelancers looks at some terms of engagement that need to be considered in a Contract *for* Services. Professional advice should be sought.

7 Your network

Keep in touch with your colleagues, and make use of the network.

 It can take effort to keep in touch with your colleagues, but an online business and employment-oriented service like LinkedIn, based in California, provides a venue for professional networking, including employers posting jobs and job seekers posting their CVs.

 Do not underestimate the power of the personal network. Your reputation with other professionals, businesses and among parents and carers can be the most powerful recommendation and is a free by-product.

You may also wish to consider some of the issues set out below that you may feel pertinent to your own circumstances.

As a business

If you have a more entrepreneurial streak and wish to set up a business with premises and engaging or contracting a team, there is more to running a successful business than deciding that you are capable, or that it is a good idea.

The type of issues you will need to consider:

1   Your market

As for the freelancer, dance, in all its forms, is a growing market. As well as its theatrical and artistic presentation, it covers a number of career and lifestyle choices, among them, educational, community, recreational, keeping fit, dance and older people, dance and disability, cultural, young people, health and well-being.

- Choose which market segment in which to base your business – whether by career, lifestyle choices, benefits, dance genre(s) or any combination thereof; and in what format, as a school, dance company or any other type of dance business – but ensure that your choices are sustainable, approachable, achievable and workable.

- Dance brings many benefits – among them physical activity, social interaction, mental stimulation, discipline, artistic expression and understanding, and motivation.

- Some dance is more popular than others. Traditionally, ballet attracts girls, although boys are becoming increasingly more involved. Ballroom dancing has become even more popular because of the impact of television shows whose format is adopted around the world, while street and urban dance have grown enormously over the past decade due to popular culture. Contemporary dance has had an increased interest base because it is seen as accessible as well as being the chosen genre for some national dance curriculums. Video sharing websites such as YouTube help to grow both participation and audiences.

2   Your competitors

You must be aware of what is happening in your chosen field. Dance is not a new product or service, but your approach can be. You will be sharing the market with other businesses. You should get to know your competitors. Many dance businesses or schools operate successfully within the same area or market, *i.e.,* there is space for all.

- The dance press and dance exhibitions can showcase competing businesses. Online directories can be a source of competitors, as are the more traditional Yellow Pages/Yell print directories or local equivalent.

- Dance Awarding Organisations (DAOs) which register teachers can offer "Find a Teacher" on their websites, which can be a way to find out what other dance businesses are in your catchment, zip or postcode areas.

Competitors need not be competitors. You can collaborate with other dance businesses *e.g.,* by offering classes complementary to theirs as a feeder, different dance genres, or different age groups, co-producing shows or providing retail opportunities.

3 Your customers

If you are starting a business, you should identify your target customer base and catchment area.

You should be able to find out the total population in your potential catchment area and the breakdown by gender and age. Compare previous periods to see if and how the catchment area is contracting or expanding, and compare it to the size of similar businesses already operating in your chosen area.

Age division can be fluid according to perception and type of business. For a dance school, potential customers or your market segmentation could fall into the following groups:

○ New-born

○ Pre-school

○ Young people

○ Young adults and adult learners

○ Older learners

○ Cross-generational

Businesses can create a safe and welcome place for customers to express themselves through dance. Compassion should be used when exploring the best options and discussing issues such as preferred name, attire, washroom and changing facilities, appropriate examinations, etc.

 Dance schools are already accepting transgender and gender-diverse students and adults for class, and some Dance Awarding Organisations are allowing transgender to choose the appropriate examination.[2] [3]

4 Your location

The physical location of your dance business can be critical if you rely on customers attending on site. In practice, it may be difficult to find an optimum site and a compromise solution may need to be found.

---

[2] Includes people whose gender identity or gender expression is the opposite of their assigned sex (trans men and trans women)

[3] (Howard, 2016)

- 🔅 Suitable venues often hire out to more than one dance business. Ensure that the property owner has no restrictions on hiring to same-activity competitors, and that the other dance activity is happy with the arrangement.

- 🔅 Some customers can view dance classes as a *Monday* or *Wednesday* activity for their children rather than having loyalty to a particular school. This perception can potentially help a new school share premises, as classes held on days not covered by the existing school would not necessarily be competing.

The virtual location is also important, as you will want customers to find you easily on the internet.

5 Your product or service

Determine why customers would come to you. What is your product differentiation? For a dance school, a non-exhaustive list of potential products and services could include:

○ Choice of dance genres: ballet, contemporary, modern, jazz, tap, urban, classical Indian, ballroom, Scottish, musical theatre.

○ Choice of class: group, mixed, boys, dance and disability, adult learners, older learners, special educational needs.

○ Choice of ability: pre-school, graded, vocational graded, beginner, intermediate, advanced.

○ Choice of services: dance classes, internal school assessments, private lessons, mentoring, seasonal activities (summer schools), workshops, external Dance Awarding Organisation examinations, studio rental.

○ Choice of staff: you and your team.

If you are starting your own school, your teaching qualifications may initially limit what you can teach, but this can be resolved by employing or contracting a teacher or teachers to fill the gap or acquiring additional qualifications.

- 🔅 Contracting a teacher might be you if you have made a choice to be a freelancer on your own account.

- 🔅 The acquisition of additional skills or qualifications would satisfy a requirement of any professional teaching body that required annual continuing professional development (CPD).

6 Pricing

Product pricing should cover your business costs while allowing you to make a profit. For a dance school, the product price would be the prices of classes or other services; for a dance theatre, the seat cost; and for a dance conference or course, the event cost.

Prices will be based upon costs and your overall income needs, but you should also be aware of what your competitors are charging. No two pricing schemes are the same and there will be valid reasons why fees differ between one business and another. If your prices are higher, ensure that you can justify them to yourself and your customers.

 Do not set prices too low, as you will want to differentiate from other products, services or business.

In writing the Business Plan, identify any Unique Selling Propositions (USPs) that will mark you out from your competitors.

 Revisit your budget if you feel your prices are out of line with the competition.

 Some schools offer external examinations at an additional cost. Ensure that payees are aware of how and what you charge for all your services and products.

Pricing is a function of volume and costs. If student numbers need to be increased to raise income, you cannot always rely on retaining 100% of the extra income. There is a marginal rate of return. Extra students can require additional space, additional teaching, additional administration, etc. These factors may increase your total costs and reduce the additional income.

 If you need to raise income and student numbers, calculate the greatest number of students that you can add to your existing classes without increasing studio space, costs, teaching hours, and without compromising quality.

7 Your resources

Ensure that you are up-to-date with your skills and if you are starting a business, ensure your:

○ Premises are up-to-date, fit-for-purpose, and are appropriate for the expected number of customers.

○ Team are qualified, adhere to their professional body's Code of Conduct and Professional Practice, and are DBS checked (or equivalent).

○ Team are imbued with the ethos of the school, demonstrate integrity and present a unified front to customers and suppliers.

Determine the extent to which technology might be changing the dance industry and how you can use it to your best advantage.

8 Your marketing

When dealing with your marketing environment, be proactive.
You can create the kind of environment you will prosper in and become more efficient. Place equal emphasis on both the micro- and macroenvironment and react appropriately to changes.

Consider the best method of bringing your business to the marketplace, whether by social media, or by more traditional advertising and promotional materials, or a combination of both. Research which option has the best outcomes. As for a freelancer:

- Do not underestimate the power of the personal network. Your reputation with other businesses and among parents and carers can be the most powerful recommendation and is a free by-product of a good business.

- Do not underestimate the impact of social media. Social media can be used for both good and bad comments by your customers, parents and carers.

- Keep in touch with your colleagues through online business and employment-oriented services like LinkedIn, based in California, which provides a venue for professional networking, including employers posting jobs and job seekers posting their CVs.

Getting help

You will need to learn quickly about many areas of business with which you might not be familiar. Many countries have local enterprise or government agencies, business chambers, small business agencies or similar which will provide general free online advice on setting up in business, resolving problems, training and raising finance.

Governments are developing single points of contact for government services and other valuable information. Gov.uk[4] is a United Kingdom public sector information website, created by the Government's Digital Service to provide a single point of access to HM Government services.

Your professional body may provide networking opportunities with like-minded individuals or those who have been in the business for a while. Trade

[4] (HM Government, 2018)

shows also provide networking opportunities, as well as independent dance teacher networks. Social media offers a plethora of networking sites.

The internet has a wealth of information regarding tax advice and business start-up issues relating to most countries. The internet also has helpful information regarding working in or relocating to other countries, as well as templates, agreements and contracts that can be adapted to suit your individual needs. Internet search engines make finding free data easy, but you should be aware that not all sites are reliable.

Ensure that any professionals you consult for advice and help have been properly accredited, chartered, registered, certified or regulated by their own professional or parent body. Most professionals belong to their registration body and it is strongly recommended that checks are made and references taken up. You should discuss the scope of any work you are taking advice on or contracting for, ensure that they are familiar dealing with start-ups the size of yours and that everyone is clear about the outcomes.

1   Accountants

Accountancy firms, business consultancies and government agencies can typically provide initial and on-going advice regarding:

✓ Which type of business structure is most appropriate

✓ Approaching your bank manager

✓ Preparing a Business Plan

✓ Bookkeeping and record keeping

✓ Setting up and preparing business accounts

✓ Tax liability – direct and indirect

✓ Applying for grants

✓ Cash flow and budgeting forecasting

✓ Valuing a business

✓ Tax registration and annual tax returns

✓ Business registration, licences and permits

✓ General business advice

Not all accountants have formal qualifications and not every firm offers all these services. The Consultative Committee of Accountancy Bodies (CCAB) in the United Kingdom, which represents international accounting bodies, can assist.[5] Ensure that any professional you consult

[5]   (Consultative Committee of Accountancy Bodies (CCAB), 2018)

or contract has initials after their name that you can check, and references you can take up. A bookkeeper can take on your bookkeeping records. They need to be competent rather than a fully qualified accountant, but they may not necessarily be able to interpret your figures for you.

Accountancy firms often provide bookkeeping services. Alternatively, franchises like TaxAssist, based in the United Kingdom, can offer accounting and bookkeeping services to the small business sector.

2   Lawyers

Solicitors, attorneys, advocates and law firms can typically advise on:

✓ Legal formation of a company

✓ Partnership agreements

✓ Buying an existing business

✓ Buying premises

✓ Leasing agreements

✓ Employment legislation

✓ Contracts *of* and *for* service

✓ Trade mark, patent and copyright laws

✓ Business advice

Solicitors, attorneys, advocates and law firms can specialise in different branches of the law, or, if big enough, have sufficient partners to deal with different areas. The Law Society of England and Wales and the Law Society of Scotland, the professional associations that represent and govern the lawyers' profession in England and Wales, and Scotland respectively, have a "Find a Solicitor" service.[6] [7] You should ensure that when you approach a legal firm they are capable of dealing with your particular issues and, as with accountancy firms, take references.

3   Bankers

Banks, government agencies and business advisers can assist with new business funding, start-ups and expansion. They can provide useful brochures, leaflets and information packs. It can be better to separate your business and personal banking between different banks so that one does not influence the other.

Consider trying other banks before approaching your own, just to gain experience in presentation.

---

[6]   (The Law Society of England and Wales, 2018)

[7]   (The Law Society of Scotland, 2018)

4 Financial advisers

Financial advisers can advise on financing business as well as finding sources of funds. These types of advisers are more often used for company flotations and initial public offers (IPOs).

5 Chartered surveyors

Surveyors, realty firms and estate agencies can assist when buying, renting, leasing, renewing, or giving notice on premises.

6 Insurance brokers

Insurance brokers can advise on appropriate insurance policies. The British Insurance Brokers' Association (BIBA), an organisation representing the interests of insurance brokers, intermediaries and their customers in the United Kingdom, may assist in finding a suitable broker through their Find Insurance service.[8]

7 Online consultants

Web designers and online media consultants can assist in developing, designing and optimising your website, social media platforms, email letterhead, online advertising, Pay-per-Click, mobile apps and other tools. Web designers are often chosen by word-of-mouth, reputation and preference.

8 IT consultants

IT specialists and database experts can assist with advice on hardware, software, networks, databases, accounting packages, websites and integration. New packages, payment platforms and systems are being developed all the time. Accounting packages, such as Sage, NetSuite, QuickBooks, Salesforce and Xero, are often integrated with app-based products that accept and process payments. These packages may be suitable for your business and be compatible with your database.

9 Mentors

Some long-established business owners may be willing to act as mentors, or are recognised as accredited CPD providers. Dance Awarding Organisations often have a regional network of teachers who meet regularly and can assist a new teacher or owner.

The next chapter helps you to put the fruits of your research and the "who, what, why and where" of your ideas into a Business Plan.

---

[8] (British Insurance Brokers Association (BIBA), 2018)

CHAPTER 3

WRITING A BUSINESS PLAN

KEY POINTS

Structure and contents   Executive Summary   Detailed Plan   Presentation

Once you have identified the "who, what, why and where" of your business idea, you can start to write your Business Plan.

A Business Plan can play a key role in the start-up, restructure, or expansion of a business. It defines your objectives, strategies, marketing; projects income from fees and operating expenditure, and describes how you plan to achieve these goals. It is your Master Plan.

There are two good reasons why you need one:

- A demonstration of the viability of the business to potential partners, funders and investors.
- A means of engaging the support of your customers, suppliers and potential employees.

You should personally write the Business Plan as you had the idea, did the research and you know what you are proposing.

- Use plain or simple language
- Be concise in your Executive Summary to enable the reader to understand what your business is all about after a quick glance.
- Be specific in the Detailed Plan to provide a genuine overview of what you are embarking on.
- Be clear about your understanding of the target market.
- Be realistic about the finances, the viability of the business and the return on your time and investment.

This chapter explores the structure and content of a Business Plan.

Planning and building a business can be a rewarding but challenging time. Business Plans are a vision into the future, they "are inherently strategic. You start here, today, with certain resources and abilities. You want to get to a point in the future (usually three to five years out) at which time your business will have a different set of resources and abilities as well as greater profitability and increased assets. Your plan shows how you will get from here to there."[1]

"The completion of a Business Plan helps you to examine exactly where the business is today, where it could be tomorrow, and how to get there."[2]

It is a personal tool. A blueprint for running your business – providing strategy and benchmarks to help you understand your longer-term objectives and enabling you to measure progress along the way by testing the assumptions you have made. When and how you grow should form part of your business strategy – the right people, skills and resources will support your business growth.

For growing businesses, take a slow, steady, incremental approach to expansion. Start with a strong foundation upon which to build the business, undertake sound planning and set realistic goals. Growth occurs differently for every business.

Structure and contents

A Business Plan should ideally contain:

- An Executive Summary
- A Detailed Plan
- Appendices to support the detail

The ideal size of a Business Plan is thought to be between 15–25 pages, excluding the Appendices. Appendices should be kept to a minimum, be brief and to the point.

There are many formats and templates available online. For example, Palo Alto Software[3], a network and enterprise security company based in California, offers many plans, including a Dance Studio Business Plan. The Prince's Trust[4], a charity based in the United Kingdom but also delivering programmes in Australia, Canada, India, Barbados, Jordan, Pakistan and Malta, offers free Business Plan templates. Nesta, an innovation foundation

[1]   (John Rampton, 2016)
[2]   (Flood, Step 2 Meaningful Business Planning, 1993).
[3]   (Palo Alto, 2018)
[4]   (The Prince's Trust (GB), 2018)

based in the United Kingdom, provides tools and resources for download[5] and publishes a creative enterprise toolkit.[6] These, and many other templates, can help you put together your Business Plan. Find one that works for you. It will take you a few weeks to write if you are going to do it thoroughly. Some sections will be easier to complete than others.

Executive Summary

The business name and owner details should ideally be set out at the beginning of the plan, followed by the Executive Summary which should highlight and sum up the most relevant points from the Detailed Plan.

The Executive Summary should cover the following points and ideally be written and inserted after the Detailed Plan has been prepared:

○ What the business is
○ What the market is
○ What the potential is
○ What the profitability is
○ What investment is needed

The reader should be able to get a sense of the business proposal without having to read the whole document. Lenders, bank managers, funding partners and stakeholders will often make provisional judgements based on the Executive Summary.

Demonstrate that you (and your team) have the ability to manage the business and convince any funding partners and stakeholders of the existence, potential and profitability of the market and the idea and that their investment can be repaid. Convince the reader that your business will stand out from others and that it can attract customers.

The Detailed Plan of the Business Plan can then be read to confirm initial reactions or decisions.

Detailed Plan

The detail should support the Executive Summary, and can include sections on:

1 Business name, status, structure and environment
2 Products and services

---

[5] (Nesta, 2018)
[6] (Nesta, 2018)

3 Marketplace and competitors

4 Brand, sales and marketing strategies

5 Your qualifications, background and expertise

6 Your team

7 Your operations and environment

8 Financial projections

9 Financial needs, risks and requirements

10 Professional advisers and advice

Let us imagine that your business is a dance school. The points made within the sections below are for consideration, are neither exhaustive nor prescriptive, can be adapted depending on whether you are starting out, restructuring or expanding, and can be adapted for other types of business. You can determine the order in which the sections appear in the plan.

1 **Your business name, status, structure and environment**

State your trading name and describe the business clearly and concisely:

○ Set out the business objectives.

○ Start date of the business.

○ Explain what you want to do, are doing now, or plan to change or add.

○ The type of business structure you currently are, or envisage becoming.

○ The macro-/microenvironment in which your business will be located. *e.g.,* the factors, issues, challenges and relevant agencies that impact on, and influence, your business portfolio or operation internally and externally, and upon you as an individual.

2 **Your products and services**

Describe the classes and other services you will offer:

○ Dance genre, classes, private lessons, summer schools, workshops, external examinations, studio rental, etc.

○ How your classes or other services will differ or stand out from competitors.

○ How customers will gain from using your classes and other services.

○ State which classes or other services you expect to be the most profitable and why.

○ Explain what plans you have if one class or other service is more popular than others.

○ Explain how your business might recognise and react to changing customer needs.

○ Explain if your business, a particular class, or other service might benefit your customers through regulation by government or external agencies *e.g.,* external examinations regulated by a Dance Awarding Organisation; the business validated by a government agency.

3 **Your marketplace and competitors**

Describe the market in which you are offering classes and other services:

○ Primary and secondary target markets – age, gender, level, specialism, etc.

○ Location, size and catchment area of your target market.

○ Analysis of the market segment – trends, growth/decline, size, viability, seasonal factors, etc.

○ Anticipated size of your share of the target market.

○ Potential for growth.

○ Where you want to be in Years 1, 2 and 3.

○ Analysis of the buying power within or behind the market segment.

○ Source and reliability of your research.

Provide data on:

○ Direct and indirect competitors within your catchment area.

○ Analysis of that competition, including strengths and weaknesses.

○ Analysis of what you can learn and capitalise on from the competition.

○ Analysis of your typical customer.

○ Analysis of why customers may move to you and away from the competition.

○ Analysis of how you might deal with competitors losing market share to you.

○ Your Unique Selling Propositions (USP). USPs need to have the ability to retain existing, and attract new, customers.

If you are restructuring or expanding, adapt to include your achievements to date and the expertise that you bring. Explain where you anticipate the additional growth will come from and how you can harness it. (*E.g.,* new market, new product, etc.). Dance schools can grow naturally by attracting more students to existing classes, by adding extra dance classes or a new dance genre without necessarily increasing the capacity of the existing premises. An existing dance school may decide to move from rented to owned premises.

State what you believe the public perception of your existing business is. Describe the competition that may be offering similar classes and other services and how you have previously dealt with them.

The Business Plan should capitalise on your strengths and opportunities, improve perceived weaknesses, and remove or counter any threats.

 It can be useful to prepare a SWOT or TOWS analysis, jotting down your strengths (S), weaknesses (W), opportunities (O) and threats (T) and document these in your Business Plan. By analysing the external environment (threats and opportunities) and your internal environment (weaknesses and strengths), you can use the findings to determine the strategy of your business, product or service, or team. You can also use the findings to think about a process, a marketing campaign, or developing your own skills and experience.

 You can also apply a SWOT (TOWS) analysis to your competitors although your knowledge of them may be more superficial.

Strengths (Threats)	**Weaknesses** (Opportunities)
(**Weaknesses**) Opportunities	(Strengths) Threats

A PESTEL analysis, as explained in *Chapter 2: Becoming Self-Employed* in the section on Environmental factors, can be used as a diagnostic tool to identify threats and weaknesses from the SWOT (TOWS) analysis. It can help to give a better understanding of the strategic choices you face. (Remember that strategy is the art of determining how you will win in business and life.) It can help you ask, and answer, the following questions:

Table 3.1: SWOT and TOWS questions

SWOT	TOWS
How do you:	How do you:
Make the most of your strengths?	Manage your threats?
Circumvent your weaknesses?	Capitalise on your opportunities?
Capitalise on your opportunities?	Circumvent your weaknesses?
Manage your threats?	Make the most of your strengths?

If you have been previously employed, and you want to set up your own business in an area where your former employer is already doing business, you should ensure that your employment contract does not contain a noncompete clause (NCC), or a covenant-not-to-compete clause (CNC).

These terms are used in contract law where one party (usually the employee) agrees not to enter into or start a similar profession or trade in competition against another party (usually the employer). These are also known as "restrictive covenants" or "restraint of trade".

The use of such clauses is generally based upon the possibility that an employee, on leaving an employer, might begin working for a competitor or start a business. In doing so, they could gain competitive advantage by exploiting confidential information regarding their former employer's operations or sensitive information such as customer lists, business practices, upcoming products, or marketing plans. The law will generally protect the employer if, in fact, protection is necessary, but will protect the employee if the clause is found to be onerous and too restrictive.

You should seek specialist legal advice if you are affected as an employer, employee or freelancer by such a clause. In some countries, this advice may be provided by a specialist organisation similar to the Advisory, Conciliation and Arbitration Services (ACAS)[7], an organisation in the United Kingdom that provides information, advice, training, conciliation and other services for employers and employees to help prevent or resolve workplace problems.

4 **Your brand, sales and marketing**

Describe your:

- O Brand image.
- O Marketing strategy.
- O Proposed pricing structure.
- O Strategy for introductory and continuing promotions/discounts.
- O Whether you intend to launch classes in phases, and how long start-up or expansion will take.
- O Analysis of anticipated attendance per class or activity, costs and profitability.

If you are restructuring and expanding, adapt to include what you do already, where you want to grow and why.

---

[7] (ACAS, 2018)

Describe how you intend to sell the business to your chosen market segment, and why you have chosen these methods:

○ How you plan to position your classes and other services – price, quality, frequency.

○ Who is your target market – the payee/end user?

○ How you will promote and sell the business or individual classes and other services – via a website, social media, public relations, direct mail, flyers, email, face to face, word of mouth, etc.

○ How you will use your website and social media to benefit the customer, and how the customer will be able to use your website and social media to benefit the business.

○ How you might use technology to help your business.

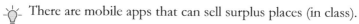 There are mobile apps that can sell surplus places (in class).

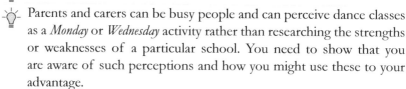 Parents and carers can be busy people and can perceive dance classes as a *Monday* or *Wednesday* activity rather than researching the strengths or weaknesses of a particular school. You need to show that you are aware of such perceptions and how you might use these to your advantage.

If you are restructuring and expanding, adapt to include what you do already, and how you will improve on it.

5 Your qualifications, background and expertise

Explain the background to your business idea, including your qualifications, education and training, teaching specialisms, expertise and experience. Sell yourself; indicate what your personal investment might be. This could be the amount of time you intend to devote, a skills upgrade, an initial lump sum investment, or recognition that your earnings in the first few years will be low.

○ The roles you will be covering – class teaching, marketing, finance, administrative tasks.

Explain how the business will manage if you fall ill or are injured. You will need to describe how these roles will be filled and whether the person doing this is capable of "filling your shoes".

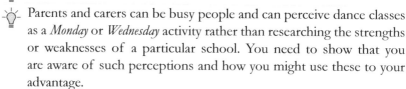 The self-employed tend to cover a myriad of roles, not only teaching class but also marketing and administration. It can be tough at the beginning.

If you are restructuring or expanding, include all of the above points, as well as how long the business has been in existence and whether you anticipate any change in the role you play. *E.g.,* you may have decided to undertake more administrative work and hand over teaching to members of your team.

6 **Your team**

Outline who you wish to employ, are in partnership or collaborating with:

- The number of individuals on the team, and details of their qualifications, skills and abilities, experience, and their readiness to join you in the business.
- Their roles, what they will contribute and how they complement your own contribution.

- Parents often do not realise that dance teachers should be properly qualified and any marketing should stress this aspect.

- Professionalism and trustworthiness will mark you out to students, parents and carers, and investors.

Describe how you intend to manage the school with your team. This could include roles, responsibilities and accountability reporting lines.

- Use a visual tool such as a flowchart or organogram.

7 **Your operations and environment**

Explain how the business will operate and how classes and other services will be delivered to the customer:

- Type of premises: rented or owned, security, facilities, length of rental period, break clauses, rent reviews.
- Pros and cons of the chosen location.
- Dance equipment: barres (mobile/fixed), mats, audio-visual and video equipment, etc.
- Office equipment: tables, chairs, laptops, PCs.
- Systems: school database, accounting software, payment platforms, mobile apps.

- Ensure that any database you purchase or subscribe to is able to cope with different or multiple payees. It would be reasonable to expect that adults and young adults will be the end user and the payee; but in the case of young children, the parent or carer would be the payee. However, in some cases the payee could be a grandparent, a divorced parent, a trust or fund, or any combination thereof.

- Administrative staff needs.

○ Frequency of classes and potential timetable.

○ Regulatory issues.

○ Local council requirements.

○ Policies: codes of conduct, health and safety, safeguarding young people and vulnerable adults, data protection, equality and diversity, insurance, trade mark protection, licensing, use of music, etc.

8 **Financial projections**

Demonstrate financial viability. Use budgets, costing and break-even to prepare your financial statements and cash flow. Establish your day-to-day operating costs, break-even, start-up capital and profit. These are business tools that can help translate your plan into financial numbers and give an indication of how the business will survive and move forward.

 Refer to *Chapter 6: Using Financial Tools*.

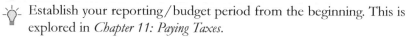 Establish your reporting/budget period from the beginning. This is explored in *Chapter 11: Paying Taxes*.

A summary of the financial figures (ideally for each of the first three years of trading) should be in the midsection of the Business Plan with the detail set out in Appendices.

 Keep the presentations clear and simple.

 The financials in the Detailed Plan and the Appendices can be simplified by summarising expenditure under sub-headings.

The financials should be accompanied by a list of key assumptions. Consider the following points:

For Income and Expenditure projections:

✓ Attendance, fee levels, number of classes

✓ Class breakdown by individual streams and genre

✓ Income calculation (sales volume)

✓ All types of expenditure

✓ Earnings drawdown

✓ Other income-producing activities

✓ Effect of consumption taxes on your business

For calculating Cash Flow from the Income and Expenditure projections:

✓ Invoicing frequency – per week, month, term, or walk-in

✓ Payment methods – cash, mobile, web, factoring

✓ Payment incentive plans

✓ Time lags between invoicing and collection

✓ Attainment of volume and income projections

✓ Regular and irregular payment pattern, both business and personal

✓ Existing business loans

✓ Third party investment already agreed

✓ Own investment

 Make all of your projections as realistic as possible.

9 Financial needs, risks and requirements

Arising out of the Income and Expenditure and Cash Flow statements, you should be able to project the funding requirements for the business.

Ensure that your initial cash flow pattern, including any funding, is robust enough to carry you through uneven cash periods and through a whole year and not just term time. Starting out, restructuring and expanding can come at an increased cost for a period, before income catches up.

⚬ Owners of dance schools need to realise that activities based on traditional school terms only bring income into the business for a 36 to 40-week period.

You need to show how your school is going to be funded and by how much. This is what any potential funder or stakeholder is primarily interested in. Projections should illustrate how you have arrived at any potential request for funding, whether long or short term.

A potential funder does not necessarily need to be a bank or another type of formal lender; it could be a spouse, friend, or partner, but that person will need to be reassured that you have carefully thought out your new business. These sources are explored in *Chapter 10: Funding*. **Irrespective of the source**, a legal agreement should be drawn up for any type of lending.

○ Indicate how much finance you require, the time frame, in what form – *e.g.,* fixed interest loan, loan drawdown, line of credit, and overdraft.

○ Indicate what the funds will be used for *e.g.,* equipment, premises, working capital (financing stock, debtors, general cash flow).

Use the cash flow exercise as a form of risk assessment to determine the extent of funding required in the early years if a shortfall arises because your projected volume and income does not materialise. Assessing risk will help you minimise problems and help build up your credibility with any investor or bank. Calculate "What if" scenarios:

○ What (happens) if budgeted class attendance is slower than expected?

○ What (happens) if customer payments are slower than expected?

○ What (happens) if costs escalate?

○ What (happens) if you fall ill or are injured?

○ What (happens) if a key employee leaves?

Improving cash flow can be achieved by using factor services where a company will assume the risk of collection and pays a fixed percentage of invoiced value upfront to the business, and pays the balance less a fee at a later date.

10 Professional advisers and advice

Include professional advisers you have consulted, the type of advice you have received and those you have retained. These could include a teaching mentor or the previous owner (if applicable).

Presentation

Business Plans should ideally be marked confidential, be well spaced out and presented in a folder or electronically, or both. If you are concerned about competitors getting a copy, give each copy a unique watermark and include a simple non-disclosure agreement at the beginning of the folder for each recipient to sign, and password protect electronic copies. Keep a control list of who has a copy.

Practice your delivery with your mentor. Retain the main elements in your mind so that you can quote at will. Be clear what you want to say and why. Be confident in delivery; listen and respond well to questions asked.

You may decide at the end of writing the plan that the business is too risky and that it might be more prudent to follow the freelance option, or you now have a plan to follow and move forward. In either event, the exercise can be worth the outcome.

In the following chapters, some of the issues in choosing a business name, the right structure, and some of the financial tools available are explored.

CHAPTER 4

CHOOSING A BUSINESS NAME

KEY POINTS

Business name   Trade marks   Registered trade mark   Unregistered mark
Misrepresentation or passing off   Domain name   Tag lines   Being noticed

---

Whether you are operating as a freelancer or as a business, the right business name, product name or company name can be crucial to the success of the business.

Intellectual property can be harder to protect than material assets. Your business name and logo are examples of intellectual property assets. They are an inclusive part of operating a successful business and are good marketing and selling tools.

A business name and a trade mark have different purposes, and protect the business in different ways.

A business name primarily identifies a business. Registering a business name does not always confer the exclusive right to use the name as a business name. It is not always sufficient to register a business name at the appropriate office or even to register a name as an internet domain, and then just hope for the best.

A trade mark legally protects a business name and allows the owner to take legal action to stop others from trading with it. A trade mark grants full rights over a word or symbol, such as a logo, or both. Trade marks usually last for a period of ten years before renewal for a further ten years.

This chapter explores the issues relating to business names, registered trade marks, unregistered marks and domain names.

Business name

A business operates, and is usually connected to a tax identity, under its business name. Requirements differ from country to country. Some jurisdictions do not require a formal registration; others do. Some ask owners to register a business name only if different from their given name; others ask all owners to register.

> In Jamaica, if the applicant's trade name is different from his or her given name, the trade name/business name must be registered at the Companies Office of Jamaica (COJ), under the Business Names Act.[22]

A business name does not bestow any legal rights. This means that if someone else uses your business name for their business, you do not always have the right to stop them.

It is however necessary to follow a few basic rules, whether you have to register or not. A business name cannot normally:

- Be identical, the same as, or too similar to another.
- Suggest a connection with a government or state organisation.
- Contain sensitive names or expressions unless permission has been granted.
- Be offensive.

A similar sounding name is the most common form of misrepresentation, or passing off, which is explained later in this chapter.

"Same as" names are those where the only difference to an existing name might be punctuation, a special character, or a domain indicator:

> *Danceschool UK* and *Dance School* are the *same as Danceschool. Danceschool.com* is *too similar* to *Danceschool.*

A connection with government might be, for example:

> Under Malaysia's LN 282/57 Registration of Businesses 1957 Rule 15, business names cannot be registered (except with the consent of the Minister) if the name wrongly suggests connections by including such words as "Royal" or any equivalent expression; "Federal", "State" or "National"; any words suggesting connection with any ASEAN, Commonwealth or other foreign Government, or with the United Nations, or any other international organisation; "Chartered" or any words suggesting connection with any Society or body incorporated by Royal Charter; "Association", "Union", "Foundation", "Trust", "Forces", "Co-operative", "International" or any equivalent expression, among other restrictions.[23]

---

[1] (Companies Office of Jamaica, 2018)
[2] (Companies Commission of Malaysia (SSM), 2018)

If you are a freelancer, you can trade under your given name or under a different name. If you decide to have a different name, you can disclose it in formal documents, stationery and correspondence as:

> Mr J Smith t/a *Danceschool* or dba *Danceschool*
> where t/a is short for "trading as" and dba is short for "doing business as".

If you are incorporating yourself or your business as a company, company formation officials will verify the company name prior to registering a new business. In reviewing the company's documentation, officials will check whether the name is already in use and whether the use of words is permitted.

As a general starting point when choosing a business name, you should conduct or commission a search to determine whether anybody is already using the same or a similar name. Trade mark attorneys and solicitor firms can arrange this.

The concept of whether goodwill may exist in the seller and the business name is discussed in *Chapter 19: Buying (or Selling) a Business*. If you are buying a business, you should consider whether you want to retain the existing business name or change it. Business names can be both rational and emotional, the rational being derived from convenience, value, reliability, while the emotional might be tied to personality and customer care.

Trade marks

Trade marks are registered in specific countries. In the European Union (EU), it is possible to register a European Union trade mark (EUTM) which covers all the member states. If you wish to ensure your business name cannot be taken or used by anyone else, you should protect the name by means of a formal trade mark registration. This will provide you with the exclusive right to stop others from using your business name in relation to the classes of goods and/or services for which it has been registered. You should note, however, that others might have prior rights to your desired trade mark, which, even if not identical, could mean that you cannot use your trade mark without risking infringing third party trade marks. This might require you, for example, to enter into a co-existence agreement or to reconsider your business name to avoid infringing third party rights.

Two symbols can be used as notice of your rights. The ® symbol puts third parties on notice of registered rights, while the ™ symbol puts third parties on notice of unregistered or common-law rights. The former mark ® relates to a full registration; the latter mark ™ relates to a business name that is in use but not registered, or in use but pending registration and is an unregistered brand or mark.

Registered trade mark ®

Trade mark attorneys and solicitor firms can help in the registration process, which requires filing the trade mark application, conducting a trade mark search, completing the trade mark application and liaising with relevant authorities during the application process. If the chosen trade mark is already in use, or too similar to another trade mark, the filing process should discover this if you request a clearance search to be conducted in advance of filing the application.

A registered trade mark can be denoted by the symbol ®:

> If your business was trading as *Danceschool* and this was accepted as a registered trade mark, you could denote it as *Danceschool* ® on letterheads, marketing literature, websites, etc., subject to jurisdiction law.

In certain jurisdictions the use of the ® symbol can result in an offence, while in the United Kingdom it is not necessary to show these symbols.

There are currently 45 international classes, established by the Nice Classification (NCL), under which a business name can be protected as a trade mark.[3] These are an international classification of goods and services, which are updated annually. It is possible to register a trade mark for a limited number of classes, while another user can use a similar or identical trade mark for an unrelated class and potentially not infringe the trade mark, because the class is different. This is a technical area of the law and the specific circumstances of each case will determine whether the use of an identical or similar trade mark infringes a pre-existing trade mark. You should seek specialist legal advice if you are concerned about infringing a pre-existing business or trade mark.

Generally, a dance school might register its business name as a trade mark under Class 41, which covers education and training. If you have additional sources of income through merchandising and selling your own material, you might wish

---

[3]   (HM Government, 2018)

to trade mark the business name under Class 9, which covers CDs and DVDs, Class 16 for written instructional material, and Class 25 for clothing:

- Class 41 – Education, Entertainment and Sport Services

  Education; providing of **training**; entertainment; sporting and cultural activities.

- Class 9 – Computers and Scientific Devices

  Scientific, nautical, surveying, photographic, cinematographic, optical, weighing, measuring, signalling, checking (supervision), lifesaving and teaching apparatus and instruments; apparatus and instruments for conducting, switching, transforming, accumulating, regulating or controlling electricity; apparatus for recording, transmission or reproduction of sound or images; magnetic data carriers, **recording discs; compact discs, DVDs and other digital recording media**; mechanisms for coin-operated apparatus; cash registers, calculating machines, data processing equipment, computers; computer software; fire-extinguishing apparatus.

- Class 16 – Paper Goods

  Paper and cardboard; **printed matter**; bookbinding material; photographs; stationery and office requisites, except furniture; adhesives for stationery or household purposes; artists' and drawing materials; paintbrushes; **instructional and teaching materials**; plastic sheets, films and bags for wrapping and packaging; printers' type, printing blocks.

- Class 25 – Clothing

  Clothing, footwear, headgear.

Always obtain legal advice if another party uses your trade mark without obtaining prior consent from you.

Unregistered mark™

It is possible to use a brand or mark that has not been registered as a trade mark. Unregistered brands are denoted by the symbol ™. There is no legal obligation to register a trade mark before using that brand name or logo. Applications to register a trade mark can be filed at any time, even several years after starting use of a brand.

> If your business was trading as *Danceschool* and this was an unregistered trade mark, the owner could denote it as *Danceschool*™ on letterheads, marketing literature, websites, etc.

The use of the ™ symbol to denote your unregistered brand is usually to put third parties on notice that you consider your brand as your proprietary mark. If you have acquired sufficient goodwill in your brand, you may have a right of legal action in passing off in the event that someone else uses the same mark. It can also indicate that you are in the process of registering the mark as a trade mark and giving notice of your rights.

Conduct some due diligence to determine whether there are any pre-existing third party rights that are identical or similar to your chosen business name whether you register a trade mark or not. Either way, you may find yourself on the wrong end of a "cease and desist" letter claiming trade mark infringement or *passing off*.

The cost of registering a trade mark can deter individuals, but the process need not be unduly expensive if a sensible approach is taken as to what to register as a trade mark. Indeed, it is possible to do some research in advance of engaging trade mark attorneys or solicitor firms by checking trade mark registers and performing internet searches[4] as to whether your chosen business name or a similar name is already being used by someone else.

Misrepresentation or passing off

You should be aware that others might try to pass themselves off as your business. If a competitor has created potential confusion, intentionally or not, and their customers could mistake another business for yours, this could be seen as *passing off*. *Passing off* is an actionable cause of action against third parties.

The most common form of *passing off* is by using a similar-sounding name. One business may have built up a good reputation, but another business could trade using a similar-sounding name, perhaps with a slightly altered spelling or change that most customers would not notice. This can be costly in terms of business and reputation, causing a successful business to fail. It does not have to be intentional for legal action to be taken.

Similarities in the use of designs, such as a logo, product shape, style, or colour, may also amount to *passing off*. Other examples of *passing off* could be print and online advertising (including website keywords and search engine adverts), billboards, or similar-sounding voiceovers on local radio – anything that makes a business too similar that could cause confusion to customers and redirect business elsewhere.

---

[4] (HM Government, 2018)

In the United Kingdom *passing off* is a common law action that protects unregistered brands. It is based on the common-sense notion that it is an "an offence for one trader to misrepresent his goods (or services) as those of another, and so deceive customers into purchasing his goods (or services) when they thought they were purchasing those of another". For example:

> Two dance businesses may have inadvertently chosen the same or a similar name. The first business has been successfully established for many years under an unregistered brand of *TDA* or *Thom's Dance Academy*; the second business set up recently as *TDA Dance*. The owner of the first could argue that the second is *passing off* their business name, because it is very similar.

It is not necessary for a brand to be registered before it can be used as the basis of a *passing off* action, but to prove *passing off*, three elements must be substantiated by evidence:

● **Goodwill** owned by a trader: *e.g.,* showing that a brand, mark, business name, or business has an established reputation.

● **Misrepresentation:** *e.g.,* demonstrating that a misrepresentation has taken place or is likely. This requires that the mark in question must be sufficiently similar to the mark of the claimant for a customer to be deceived.

● **Damage to goodwill**: *e.g.,* proving that there is a likelihood of damage to the established business because of the deception.

The cost of a *passing off* court action is usually more costly than a trade mark infringement action, as the evidential burden is usually higher. Whether an action is ultimately successful depends on the facts of a particular case. It can provide, however, a useful remedy when a mark has not been registered but has substantial use and an established reputation.

Passing off is likely to be difficult to establish if any of the following conditions exist:

○ There is a partnership dispute.

○ An existing trade mark has been copied.

○ There is a contract dispute.

○ A conflict exists between previous business partners, employees, employers, or any other business-related dispute.

○ A business-related conflict between relatives.

○ A disputed domain name.

Common law and the right of action in *passing off* do not exist in every jurisdiction, although there can be an alternative cause of action in unfair competition in certain jurisdictions. Appropriate legal advice should always be sought when considering what rights you may have.

Domain name

It is common for a domain name to be the same as, or similar to a business name, brand name or other business identifier. Domain names and trade marks can sometimes seem similar; however, they are different. Unlike trade marks, domain names are global, unique by nature and cannot be shared between two websites. It is possible that two exist but with different domain extensions.

A domain name is used to locate and bring users to a specific website or place on the internet. It is a unique string of letters that forms part of an internet address. It can be your trade mark, name, product, service or strapline.

A domain extension is the notation at the end of a web address that specifies an internet category or a country code. Examples of an internet category are **.com** for commercial, **.org** for organisation, **.gov** for government, **.edu** for educational institutions, **.dance** for dance or **.net** for a network. A country code might be **.us**, **.uk** or **.de**. The number of available internet domain extensions is increased from time to time to cater for the growth in web addresses.

In most cases, trade marking a domain name can help protect the identity, reputation and profitability of your business. Registering a domain name does not automatically give any rights over a matching trade mark.

Unfortunately, the ease of registering a domain name has led to multiple registrations of domain names identical or similar to well-known marks so that the registrant can attempt to sell them on. This is known as cyber-squatting. The law, however, tends to favour a trade mark owner.

For a domain name to be cancelled or transferred, an owner must prove that:

● The domain name is identical or confusingly similar to the trade mark
● The registrant has no right or legitimate interest in the domain name
● The domain name has been registered and is being used in bad faith

Tag lines

Sometimes the business name you choose might be complemented by a tag or strapline, which can be used on your marketing literature as a promotional tool.

Being noticed

Your business needs to be seen and your name noticed.

Your website can be the main source to promote your business. It is worth investing in a well-designed website that will draw interest. Look at other websites to get an idea what works. Twitter, Facebook, Instagram or equivalent social media can be used both as pointers to the website and as additional promotional tools.

Your business email address should ideally include your business name (@ yourbusinessname) to reinforce the message.

Merchandise, such as t-shirts and tote bags can be emblazoned with your business name and logo.

This topic is discussed more fully in *Chapter 13: Operating* in the section Bringing in the Business.

The chosen business name needs to be given an appropriate business structure, dealt with in the next chapter.

CHAPTER 5

CHOOSING A BUSINESS STRUCTURE

KEY POINTS

Types of business   Sole trader or sole proprietor   Partnership – general or simple,
limited liability, limited   Company – Ltd., Plc.   Registration as self-employed
Registration as a company   Franchising   Charitable status

If you have decided to become an employee, there is no need to worry about choosing an appropriate business structure.

However, if you have decided to become self-employed, you must think about and decide upon the most appropriate business structure. This applies equally whether you have decided to become a freelancer on your account, or a freelance business with premises and staff.

When starting up a business, careful consideration should be given to the form in which the business is to run. A limited liability company, *e.g.,* might appear to be the most attractive because of the limited liability to debt, but it is often more tax-efficient to operate a business initially as a sole trader or partnership than as a company. For new businesses, however, whether sole, partnerships or companies, lenders will often require personal guarantees, which can negate limited liability.

When a business has prospered, a change from sole trader or partnership to a company can be timed to maximise the tax benefit.

The types of business described in this chapter are those of the United Kingdom. Although similarities exist in many countries, always seek appropriate professional advice (refer to *Chapter 2: Becoming Self-Employed* in the section Getting help) because laws, rules and regulations differ from country to country. A professional adviser will recommend the most appropriate business medium in individual circumstances.

This chapter looks at the characteristics behind different types of business structure.

Types of business

A business can be set up in a number of ways. The main types of business entity are:

- Sole trader or sole proprietor
- Partnership – general, limited liability, and limited
- Company – private and public limited liability

Before selecting the most suitable business structure, it is sensible to understand and consider the attributes of each type such as:

- ✓ Ownership and management
- ✓ Set up, records and closure
- ✓ Legality
- ✓ Risk or liability (personal versus limited liability)
- ✓ Taxation basis (personal versus corporate)

Sole trader or sole proprietor[1]

Ownership and management: A sole trader is a business formed with only one owner. You can use your own name, or choose a different name for the business.

Set up, records and closure: Generally, the set-up and administrative requirements are the simplest and least complicated. Registration requirements can differ according to the country, and can include formal registration of a business name, as well as registration with the governing tax authorities. In some countries, you have to demonstrate at least two or more sources of income if you are self-employed. Closing a business is usually straightforward.

Record keeping differs in all jurisdictions. Accounting records will need to be kept so that tax returns can be prepared and filed.

Legality: The business itself is generally not a legal entity, *i.e.,* it cannot sue or be sued in its own name, nor own or hold any property:

Your business is called *The Dance School*, but you are personally accountable.

Risk or liability: You have complete authority and control over decisions, are fully responsible for its success or failure, and are personally liable for all debts and obligations of the business. In practice, this means that personal

[1] Reference is made to sole trader only, but this includes the other descriptors.

assets, such as the family home, car, and other property, may be at risk as they could be seized to pay off outstanding debts. In the event of death, the business will pass to your estate.

Taxation basis: For a sole trader, profits are usually taxed at the personal income tax rate. You would be classified as self-employed.

Partnership

There are generally three types of partnership with varying degrees of regulation. Partnerships used to be general in nature (sharing profits and losses), but there has been a move among larger partnerships towards limited liability and limited partnerships.

General or simple partnership[2]

Ownership and management: A general partnership is a business owned by at least two individuals or companies. An upper limit on the number of partners may be legally imposed. Owners can use a combination of their own names, or choose a different business name.

A partnership marries the range of each partner's talents. Partners share the workload, the profits and the losses. Decision making can be shared, but this can lead to disagreements and, in practice, decisions are often delegated where the expertise lies:

> In a two-person partnership, one partner could be a teacher responsible for the classes, curriculum and artistic decisions; the other partner could be responsible for marketing, finance and administration.

Similarly, profits can be shared according to overall contribution and effort. You need to trust a partner, which is why a formal partnership agreement defining, inter alia, the role, responsibilities and share of profits and losses of each partner is important to avoid future disagreements. In the absence of a written agreement, disputes tend to be settled based on the conduct of involved parties, words and deeds, which represent, or allow a person to be represented as a partner and per se to become liable. This is known as partnership by estoppel, or by presumption.

Set up, records and closure: This is the quickest and easiest type of partnership to set up and administer. Registration requirements differ according to the

---

[2] Reference is made to general partnership only, but this includes the other descriptor.

country, and can include formal registration of the business name, as well as registration with the governing tax authorities.

Partnerships would normally automatically dissolve when one partner leaves the business, or dies; however, in practice most partnership agreements now provide for succession in case of death, retirement or departure.

Record keeping differs in all jurisdictions. Accounting records will need to be kept so that individual partner tax returns can be prepared and filed.

Legality: General partnerships are not a legal entity in their own right. They cannot sue or be sued in their own name and cannot own or hold any property.

> A partnership is called *The Dance School*, but the partners are personally accountable.

Risk or liability: Each partner is personally accountable for all debts and losses, and is liable for any debts incurred by the other partner(s) in the event of the other partner(s) being unable to meet their own share. This means, in practice, that personal assets, such as each partner's family home, car, and other property, may be at risk as these items could be seized to pay off outstanding debts. In the event of death of a partner, the share of the partnership at death will be owned by the deceased partner's estate.

Taxation basis: The share of profits attributable to each partner will form part of each partner's personal income and will be taxed at personal income tax rates. Each partner will be regarded as self-employed, but if one of the partners were registered as a company, that partner's taxation would be at the corporate tax rate.

Limited liability partnership (LLP)

Ownership and management: At least two individuals or companies can own a limited liability partnership. The partners can use a combination of their own names, or choose a different business name and may be required to have LLP or the local country equivalent in their business name.

LLPs combine the limited liability features of companies with the flexibility of partnerships. In some countries, LLPs may be restricted to certain professions such as accountants and lawyers.

Set up, records and closure: Changes in the composition of an LLP, such as the resignation or death of a partner, will not affect its existence, rights, or liabilities.

Record keeping differs in all jurisdictions. Accounting records will need to be kept so that individual partner and company tax returns can be prepared and filed.

Legality: An LLP is a legal entity and can sue or be sued in its own name and can own or hold any property.

> The partnership is called *The Dance School LLP*, and as a legal entity is accountable.

Risk or liability: The personal assets of the partners are protected and owners are not personally accountable for the wrongful acts of the other owners (unless subject to financial agreements taking a lien on personal assets).

Taxation basis: An individual's income from an LLP will be taxed at the personal income tax rate as if self-employed, but if one of the partners is registered as a company, that partner's taxation would be at the corporate tax rate.

Limited partnership (LP)

Ownership and management: At least one general partner and one limited partner own a limited partnership. The partners can use a combination of their own names, or choose a different business name and may be required to have LP or the local country equivalent in their business name. Investors may be more willing to join as silent partners (as the limited partner), as liability for non-general partners is limited.

Set up, records and closure: Record keeping differs in all jurisdictions. Accounting records will need to be kept so that individual partner and company tax returns can be prepared and filed.

Legality: An LP is not a legal entity. It cannot sue or be sued in its own name and cannot own or hold any property.

> The LP partnership is called *The Dance School*, which is owned by Mr, Ms, or Miss XYZ who is the general partner, and *Dancefund*, which is the limited partner.

Risk or liability: A general partner has unlimited personal liability. A limited partner is not liable for any debts and obligations beyond the agreed investment in the LP unless taking part in the management of the LP, in which case the limited liability becomes unlimited as if a general partner.

Taxation basis: An individual's income from an LP will be taxed at the personal income tax rate as if self-employed, but if one of the partners were registered as a company, that partner's taxation would be at the corporate tax rate.

Company

There are generally two types of company – private limited companies (Ltd) and public limited companies (Plc), although different acronyms may be used in other countries.

Private limited (Ltd) and public limited (Plc)

Ownership and management: A limited company is a business entity registered under the appropriate company legislation in the country. Companies can either be private (Ltd) or publicly (Plc) listed. The owners of both types of company are shareholders but the main difference is that shares in the former are traded privately, whereas shares in the latter are traded on a recognised stock exchange. Owners can be shareholders, directors or employees.

Set up, records and closure: There are more formalities and procedures to comply with when choosing to set up a company, for example the appointment of directors, annual general meetings, shareholder resolutions, audited accounts etc. There must usually be at least one shareholder and one director. These can be the same person, although, in practice, most companies have at least two directors, because banks and other financial institutions usually prefer or require two signatories.

A private limited company is usually the first choice when considering setting up a company. A company can be bought "off the shelf" from a registration agent, fast-track online service or with professional advice.

Record keeping differs in all jurisdictions. Accounting records will need to be kept so that company tax returns can be filed.

Legality: A limited company is a legal entity. It can sue or be sued in its own name and can own or hold any property.

> The company is called *The Dance School Ltd* and as a legal entity is accountable.

Risk or liability: Liability for debts is limited to the assets owned by the company if it becomes bankrupt. Each shareholder's liability for company debts is usually limited to the amount the shareholder invested in the company unless they have agreed to guarantee a debt. Directors also have duties, obligations and responsibilities which are imposed on them by legislation which if not followed properly and according to the law can lead to penalties and disqualification.

Taxation basis: Income earned by a company is taxed at the corporate tax rate. Income earned by employees would be taxed at source by the company or according to the revenue code in the country.

Registration as self-employed

As discussed in *Chapter 1: Choosing your Options*, self-employed persons can also be known as sole traders, sole proprietors, freelancers, freelance contractors, independent contractors, independent or contract workers.

Appendix 1 lists the descriptor for sole traders or sole proprietors in other countries.

If you have decided to set up as a sole trader working on your own account; a sole trader on your own account and engaging employees; or in a partnership of two or more, there is no need to register a business name in the United Kingdom, although the decision will lie with you. The only form of "registration" is a requirement to inform the authorities, who will issue a TIN (Tax Identification Number) which is known in the United Kingdom as a UTR (Unique Taxpayer Reference).

Appendix 2 lists some of the tax identification names (TIN) used around the world.

HM Revenue and Customs (HMRC) is the department of the UK Government responsible for the collection of taxes; other countries have their own authorities. HMRC requires you to complete a Form CWF1, which is a multipurpose form, used for self-employment, national insurance and VAT purposes. Forms can be obtained online or through your local revenue office. There is a three-month time limit for completion of the form.

HMRC will need to be satisfied that you will be self-employed; once registered, HMRC provides help and support.

Registration as a company

Sometimes individuals prefer to limit their personal risk and set up a limited company. If you decide to set up as a company, you will need a set of Memorandum and Articles of Association, which will detail the objectives of the company, along with other statutory requirements under the law. It is often possible to buy a company "off the shelf" with standard objectives, but these and the name can be changed to suit your particular business. The company will need to be registered with Companies House, the United Kingdom's Registrar of Companies, and with HMRC as a taxable entity, for the purposes of corporation tax, consumption tax and personal tax for your employees.

Franchising

Existing sole traders, partnerships or limited companies that have been in business for a while and are successful may consider franchising their business. A franchise is essentially a contract between the owner of a business (the franchisor) and another (the franchisee) to own and operate an additional branch or location of the existing business.

In simple terms, a franchisee pays the franchisor an upfront fee and ongoing fees based usually on a volume percentage, which will depend on the franchise, and the level of support offered.

A franchise contract needs to be clear in the obligations and rights of both parties, and usually provides details on training, support, operations, brand usage and renewal terms. Franchisors are usually expected to support franchisees with product development, marketing and advertising, promotions, operating manual, brand guidelines and other services. This is to ensure the integrity of the brand.

The British Franchising Association (BFA)[3], a voluntary self-regulatory body for the franchise sector in the United Kingdom, can provide objective advice and information to prospective franchisees and franchisors.

Charitable status

Some dance businesses, in addition to their regular business, consider setting up a charity to raise funds for good dance causes. The charity would become the promoter or presenter of a series of events, a competition, a range of merchandise or a performance and would benefit from the proceeds to satisfy its good causes.

Charity law differs from country to country and rules and regulations have to be followed. In England:

✓ Trustees must be independent

✓ Trustees are normally unpaid volunteers

✓ Trustees, employees and volunteers cannot benefit from or be paid by the charity unless authorised

---

[3] (British Franchise Association (BFA), 2018)

✓ The charity must have a single purpose recognised in law

✓ The charity cannot take part in certain political activities

✓ Strict rules apply to trading by charities

✓ The charity must provide public, up-to-date information about its activities and finances

✓ The charity must benefit a wide section of the public

These requirements can be time-consuming and there are alternatives such as:

● Working with an existing charity

● Setting up a named fund

Both of these save the time and effort of setting up and running a charity and then closing it once the original need has been met.

If you are determined to establish a charity, you need to consider that:

✓ Charities must exist only for the public benefit

✓ Charities cannot return money that has been transferred to set up the charity

✓ Charities must apply funds raised to its purpose and its purpose only

✓ Charities have separate accounting and audit rules

✓ Charities must be transparent

The Charity Commission for England and Wales, the government department that regulates registered charities in England and Wales[4] and the Office of the Scottish Charity Regulator, the Scottish administration's independent registrar and regulator of Scottish charities[5] can provide guidance on how to set up a charity.

An alternative to a Charity where an organisation might rely on grants, donations and volunteers, is a Social Enterprise which receives its income from selling goods and services and can be run by a mixture of volunteers and paid employees. These both fall into the Not-for-Profit sector and can choose from a number of different legal structures.

The next chapter looks at tools available to assist you to prepare budgets, costing, break-even, cash flow, projections and forecasts.

[4] (HM Government, 2018)
[5] (Scottish Administration, 2018)

CHAPTER 6

USING FINANCIAL TOOLS

KEY POINTS

Budgets Costing Breaking-even Cash flow Inflows Outflows Projections
and forecasts

Budgets, costing, break-even, cash flow, projections and forecasts are all methods of illustrating financial information, but all differ slightly in their use.

The words may sound challenging, but you are probably more familiar with the words than you realise – a student with a grant, an employee with a salary, or a household with a budget?

In any of these situations, you will have worked out what you can afford. If you had overspent one month, you may have had to find some form of borrowing, probably through an informal route such as your personal credit card. Then, in the ensuing months, you will have had to cut down on expenditure to cover your previous overspending. If that sounds familiar, you will have executed both a simple budget and a simple cash flow exercise.

Running a business without a budget is like driving with no idea of where you are going, or where you want to go. Running your business without forecasts is like driving with no lights on. You cannot see where you are going, or what is in front of you. A **budget** is a plan for where the business wants to go and a **forecast** is an indication of where it is actually going.

This chapter helps you to gain an understanding of the rudiments of budgeting, costing, breaking-even, cash flow, projections and forecasting.

Budgets

A budget is a quantitative expression of a financial plan for a defined period. Budgets can also be used for shorter periods, individual projects or events such as a two-week summer school or school show. It will generally include volumes and fees, costs and expenses. It might also include assets to be purchased and liabilities to be incurred. It will express your business in measurable terms.

Budgeting requires you to work out expected income and expenditure. It helps you to plan the actual business by considering how conditions might change and what steps should be taken to avoid problems before they arise. It can help with expansion plans and, more importantly, indicate that you understand your business.

The purpose of budgeting can include:

- ✓ Controlling resources
- ✓ Communicating plans
- ✓ Motivating the team
- ✓ Evaluating performance
- ✓ Measuring results and liquidity

A budget **projects** the results and liquidity and financial position. You can contrast actual performance throughout this period to the budget, and then use the financial position at that time to **forecast** what might happen. This will enable you to take appropriate action when needed. This is one of the benefits of preparing budgets personally.

Once you have started your business, get in the habit of preparing budgets each year. They can be revised during a financial year, hence terms such as *original* budget and *revised* budget.

Costing

Costing is the process by which a business estimates the costs involved in the production of a unit of output. Costing can use historical information, *i.e.,* past costs incurred by the business, to predict future cost structures, or estimated costs when the business is a start-up.

Costing allows a business to price its products and to make a more reliable estimate of sales volumes.

Costs fall into three main categories:

1 **Fixed costs** are those incurred in the normal course of business. They are "fixed" because they do not vary – irrespective of the number of hours spent teaching, the number of classes held, or the length of term.

The rent on premises can be an example of a fixed cost. These costs have to be paid regardless of how well the business is doing.

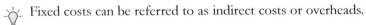 Fixed costs can be referred to as indirect costs or overheads.

2 **Semi-fixed costs** are those that have an element of fixed cost in them, but can vary according to the volume of business. These can also be known as semi-variable costs. "Semi" applies to the fact that costs may not increase until a particular threshold is reached, *i.e.,* there is an element of fixed and variable. Expenses such as utilities or telephones are good examples of semi-fixed costs as these have an element of fixed cost, the monthly rental and then an element of variable cost, the usage.

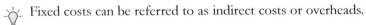 Semi-fixed semi-variable costs have elements of indirect and direct costs.

3 **Variable costs** are those that vary directly with your business. *E.g.,* if you offer dance classes, hire a studio, and employ a teacher just for those classes, the cost of the studio and the teacher's salary would be variable costs. The more classes you offer the more these costs would vary. In other words, they are in direct relation to the service you offer. If you provide each student who attends with a T-shirt and studio bag, this would be an example of variable cost.

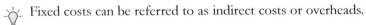 Variable costs can be referred to as direct costs.

Fixed and semi-fixed costs indicate annual overheads. Variable costs demonstrate the cost of holding an additional class. The effect of variable and fixed costs on profit can be illustrated by the following:

Example

Assume a dance school generates £50,000 of fees, has £40,000 in total costs and makes a profit of £10,000. Now, assume it doubles the number of students and, therefore, doubles its income. What happens to the profits?

Some costs are fixed and some are semi-fixed. Fixed costs generally do not increase unless a dance school has to increase its physical size and hire more teaching staff. Semi-fixed costs can increase due to additional volume but not always in proportion. Let us assume that of the original £40,000, £16,000 was variable and £24,000 was semi-fixed and fixed. The business is making £10,000 profit on sales of £50,000. Table 6.1 indicates what can happen when the fee income doubles:

Table 6.1: Effect of changing variable earnings on profits

	£	£
Fees	50,000	100,000
Variable costs	16,000	32,000
Semi-fixed costs	8,000	12,000
Fixed costs	16,000	16,000
Profit	**£10,000**	**£40,000**

Each class has the same variable cost, so variable costs double. Semi-fixed costs only increase by 50%, and fixed costs stay the same. The profit has quadrupled because productivity or throughput has substantially improved without increasing fixed costs.

This simplistic example demonstrates what happens if growth can be absorbed within an existing cost structure. This type of growth is more likely to occur when you first start out and keep growing. At a certain point in time, you will outgrow your original cost structure. Knowing your fixed, semi-fixed and variable costs will give you an understanding of the monetary effect a change in class size and attendance will have on your profits.

Table 6.2 shows some examples of typical costs (not necessarily exhaustive), their timing and cost classification.

 Classification of costs can change depending on the nature of the cost or the unit of analysis used – per business, per class, per student or circumstance. *E.g.*, teaching staff can be both *variable* and *fixed* depending on whether they are freelance and paid by the hour or employees and on the payroll. Similarly, rental can be *fixed, semi-fixed* or *variable* depending on the terms of the rental or lease agreement.

Once you determine what your costs are and where they fall, add the costs together; include a mark-up percentage to create a profit margin, then calculate the sales volume needed for the business and, from that, you could determine the pricing for your product or service.

This *cost plus* approach resolves the difficulty of determining sales volume when setting a budget.

Breaking-even

The break-even point (BEP) is the point where costs equal sales. At this point, your product or service is not making any profit, but your fixed costs

Table 6.2: Examples of classification and timing of costs

Timing	Fixed cost	Semi-fixed cost	Variable cost
Monthly			
Salary/wages	Employees		Freelancers
	Payroll tax		Musician costs
	Pension		Payroll tax
			Pension
Premises	Rental	Rental	Rental
Advertising		Advertising	
Postage		Postage	
Mobile/cell		Contract/usage	
Website costs	Broadband		Updates
Travel	Admin travel		Staff travel
Bank/cc charges		Bank/cc charges	Overdraft charges
Software subscription	Systems packages		
Loan repayments	Loan repayments		
Sundry expenses	Sundry	Sundry	Sundry
Quarterly			
Maintenance/repair		Maintenance/repair	
Fixed telephone		Rental/usage	
Utilities		Supply/usage	
Annually			
Subscriptions	Subscriptions		
Accountancy	Accountancy fees		
Insurance	Insurance premium		
Ad-hoc			
Printing		Printing	
Stationery		Stationery	
Teaching materials	Teaching materials		
Costumes/uniforms	Costumes/uniforms		
Props	Class props		
Publications	Journals/publications		
Legal costs		Retainer/advice	
Training courses	Training courses		
Promotion		Promotion/marketing	

or overheads are covered. Any excess sales over the BEP would generate a profit, while any shortfall would result in a loss.

The break-even point can be calculated using the following equation:

Gross profit = sales − variable cost
Gross profit % margin = gross profit ÷ sales × 100
Break-even point by sales = (fixed cost ÷ gross profit % margin) × 100

If your business was a dance school, the BEP equation can be refined by expressing it by the number of terms or school weeks in a year, or the number of units or revenue, which could be by either classes or students:

- Break-even point in terms or weeks = BEP by sales ÷ (terms) or (weeks); Or
- Break-even point in units = fixed cost ÷ (sales price − variable cost); Or
- Break-even point in costs/revenue = the BEP in units × by sales price.

Cash flow

Cash flow describes payments into or out of a business (or, on a smaller scale, a project or event). Costs are usually invoiced and can be paid depending on frequency monthly, quarterly, annually, or on an ad-hoc basis, although in some countries, payroll or wages can be paid every two weeks.

Cash flow projections are used to determine how well the business is creating cash and liquidity in the business, and to determine any funding requirements, scaling from a simple overdraft to a more formal loan, to avoid a potential lack of cash before it is too late.

Being profitable does not necessarily mean being liquid. A business can fail because of a shortage of cash even while it is profitable. This can be because:

✓ Inflows were not as expected, sales or attendance too low
✓ Prices are too low
✓ Outflows were underestimated, costs too high
✓ Team are not performing well
✓ Poor product or services
✓ Lack of or poor management skills
✓ Lack of or poor management information
✓ Lack of or poor financial control

Cash flow problems can result as much from mismanagement and poor decisions as from factors such as slow payment by customers or low class attendance. Any of the warning signs below can indicate that a business is experiencing cash flow problems:

✓ Overdraft limit has been reached – credit problems

✓ Difficulty in paying salaries and wages each month

✓ Difficulty in paying suppliers on time

✓ Customers are slow to pay

✓ Behind with key payments such as premises rental

✓ Lack of working capital – surviving day to day

✓ Lack of profitability – insufficient funds to support your personal needs

✓ Unable to pay for professional advice

● **Inflows**

Your estimated cash flows should be realistic, because receipt and frequency of income often differ. For example, dance school inflows can vary according to income type:

○ Fees for dance classes can be paid at the beginning of each term, or spread over the term, although some schools operate a "no payment – no place" plan.

○ Receipts from sales of merchandise are usually taken at the time of sale because it is a business-to-consumer transaction rather than business-to-business.

○ Payments for one-off workshops, events and seasonal schools are usually received in advance because places are limited and customers will want to guarantee a place.

○ Receipts from shows are both in advance and on the day.

Unrealistic assumptions will affect your projections, although once you have established a pattern of trading over time, income and receipts will be much clearer.

🔅 Your cash flow will suffer if projected payments of fees from customers are late; there is a longer lag than expected between purchases of merchandise and resale; or there is low class attendance and slow-moving stock.

Advance receipts help cash flow, but they can often disguise the fact that associated expenditure still has to be paid, and advance receipts may have been used to keep the business afloat.

It is worth investing in software that can alert parents, carers and other payees when a debt is due. Recent behavioural studies have found that the "nudge" effect with an appropriate message works.[1]

 You should have standard terms of agreement so that customers know when payments are due. (Refer to *Chapter 15: Attracting Customers.*)

● **Outflows**

Outflows or expenditure are more predictable, as shown in Table 6.2 outlining examples of typical costs, their timing and cost classification. In addition, you have control over the payment, whereas for inflows you are dependent on your customers.

Projections and forecasts

These words are often used interchangeably but there is a subtle difference. **Projections** indicate where you would like your business to be, whereas a **forecast** is an indication of where your business is actually going.

A budget is based on information from the best of your beliefs and **projects** the expected financial position of the business, results of operations and cash flows. A forecast will consider the performance to date and add the remaining budget to **forecast** where you will be at the end of a period. Your forecasting can be done for each term.

Example

A budget may project a profit of £15,000 for an academic year, but your forecast may show that you are likely to only make £10,000:

● Your **projection** of the result for the year = Budget for academic year.
● Your **forecast** for the year = Actual for two terms + remaining (or *revised*) budget for final term.

Table 6.3: Effect of forecast profit on a projected profit

	Projection £	Actual £	Forecast £	
Term 1	5,000	2,500	2,500	Actual
Term 2	5,000	3,250	3,250	Actual
Term 3	5,000		4,250	Revised
Profit	£15,000		£10,000	

---

[1] (Michael Hallsworth, 2015)

You should note that the word *revised* has been used above. This is because the first two terms' actual performance might indicate that the budget for the third term will not be met and, therefore, the original budget will need to be revised. Forecasts are a useful tool in seeing ahead in order to take affirmative or corrective action to resolve downturns or cash problems.

Projections and forecasts can apply to profit and loss statements, balance sheets and cash flow.

The next chapter puts these tools into practice.

CHAPTER 7

COSTING YOUR BUSINESS

In the previous chapter, the concepts of budgets, costing, break-even, cash flow, projections and forecasts were introduced. Costing was described as the process whereby a business estimates the costs involved in the production of a unit of output. Costing can use either historical information (past costs incurred by the business) to predict future cost structures, or estimated costs where the business is a start-up.

The primary purpose of a budget is to determine if your business is liquid, profitable, and provides you with a living, but it can be used to establish a pricing structure. In the past, the *"going rate"* or *"rule of thumb"* might have been used to calculate fees. This methodology is not necessarily wrong, and can work for manufacturers who might know the price they want to charge and then use historical costs to confirm the price.

Under-costing, under-valuing, being the cheapest or charging the same as competitors is neither cost-effective nor a guaranteed recipe for success. No two businesses are the same. Costs should be calculated first, in order to determine the level of income and profitability you want to achieve, and then the pricing structure can be calculated.

This *cost plus* approach is an alternative approach to a manufacturer who knows the price he wants to charge. It is also a more effective way of calculating sales volume at start-up than plucking figures *"out of the air"*. It also gives you the ability to ensure that the required sales volume covers the business costs and your personal needs.

This chapter applies this *cost plus* approach in a case study for a new dance school setting a **budget** to determine pricing and break-even, and calculating **cash flow** to determine shortfalls in income and funding needs.

The principles illustrated in Case Study 1[1] can be used for other types of business.

Case Study 1: Starting out

Dance schools generally receive income from class fees, sales of merchandise, and other activities such as workshops, events, seasonal schools, shows, private lessons and studio rental. Classes are held within regular timetables while other activities may occur only at specific times of the year, every other year, or outside of term times.

The main unit of output will be the cost of attending class for a term or academic year. Other events or courses can be treated separately with their own budgets.

You are going to call your dance school *XYZDanz* and you have found a studio within a community hall to rent. You have used the following facts and assumptions for the budget and Business Plan:

Administration

○ Rental: Studio, small administrative office, use of common areas such as the changing rooms, central reception, and heating and lighting.

○ Term: Hourly rental for hours contracted.

○ Rental day: Monday to Friday – 6 hours each day, Saturday – 7 hours

○ Maintenance: Responsible for the studios and common areas while you are holding your classes, as well as for minor repairs.

○ Office: Managing your business from home, with some home expenses offset as business expenses for use as an office.

○ Travel: Travelling expenses to and from your office to the studio.

You recognise you are a start-up business and although there is additional space, you have rented only one studio.

○ Dance genre: Ballet

---

[1] The figures in Case Study 1 reflect a full teaching year operating at budgeted expectation. Some of the costs, volumes, assumptions, tax treatment or benefits may not always apply to everyone's personal situation, or the jurisdiction in which a business operates. Income and costs are illustrative only and no reliance should be made on hourly rates quoted. £ Sterling is used as the currency unit (CU) but the figures can be converted to any appropriate currency unit. Rounding differences may occur in the tables and examples.

- ○ Classes: Monday to Friday – 4 classes each day; Saturday – 5 classes
- ○ Class duration: Between 45–75 minutes
- ○ Class size: Average of 15 per class
- ○ Teaching day: Monday to Friday – 4 hours each day; Saturday – 5 hours
- ○ Term time: 3 terms of 12 weeks' duration

> ·Ǭ· The average class size may sound quite ambitious but it is being used to determine pricing. If you base it on lower attendance because of the initial start-up, the fees will be calculated higher.

> ·Ǭ· Many dance schools run on a 3-term basis of 12 weeks, but you have costs for the whole year. Net income generated from 36 weeks must cover 52 weeks of your living expenses. An alternative to 3 terms of 12 weeks can be 4 terms of 10 weeks.

> ·Ǭ· Negotiate with the property owner if you can decrease or increase rental hours in your initial years. (Cash flow is explored in *Chapter 9: Analysing Cash Flow*.)

Staffing

You will undertake all the dance tuition for *XYZDanz* and will offer only classical ballet initially, in line with your dance teaching qualification. You will employ an assistant whose duties will be to register students on arrival, deal with any onsite problems, ensure students leave safely, assist in the studio when needed, and any other administrative tasks that might arise. The assistant will use the administrative office in the community hall.

You will primarily use recorded music in your classes, and live music once per term.

Volumes

There will be 900 hours of teaching a year (g), based on 25 hours of classes per week over a 36-week period:

Number of classes per week:	Hours	
Length of each class	1	
Monday–Friday – 5 days × 4 hours	20	(a)
Saturday – 1 day × 5 hours	5	(b)
Total hours per week (a + b)	25	(c)

This can be summarised as:

	Units	
Number of terms	3	(d)
Number of weeks per term	12	(e)
Number of weeks per year (d × e)	36	(f)
Number of hours per year (c × f)	900	(g)
Number of students per class	15	

Start-up costs

The rented studio has good dance flooring, has been painted, and is ready for use. A few minor renovations are required, *e.g.,* additional colour and some storage boxes. You will have to purchase furniture for the reception area and the two offices, and portable barres and dance/sound equipment, which can be stored in the administrative office on site.

You have decided to protect your business name *XYZDanz* by applying to register it as a trade mark, and have asked appropriate professional advisers to help with the lease negotiations and the Business Plan. The property owner requires a deposit of one month's rent (£1,500) which will be refundable at completion of the lease.

You have estimated start-up costs of £14,000:

Table 7.1: Case Study 1: Start-up costs

	£
Legal expenses (studio lease)	750
Consultancy fees (Business Plan)	750
Legal fees (trade mark *XYZDanz*)	1,750
Website design and costs	500
Office supplies	500
Publicity and photos	250
Signage and redecoration	1,000
Miscellaneous	1,000
Open day costs (press, taster classes, refreshments)	2,500
	£9,000

	£
Portable barres (4 × 4m)	1,500
Portable audio-visual equipment	500
Office furniture	1,500
Rental deposit	1,500
	£5,000
Total start-up costs	**£14,000**

You will require funding, as you do not have £14,000.

💡 A typical loan of £14,000 over three years can vary from a loan with an APR of 3.4% which would cost £14,724 in total (monthly repayment of £409 ×12 months × 3 years), to a loan with an APR of 9.9% which would cost £16,128 in total (monthly repayment of £448 ×12 months × 3 years).

The type of funding and annual percentage rate (APR) payable can depend on a combination of factors, *e.g.*, your credit history, the type of lender, and what guarantees or security can be offered.

Total start-up costs	£14,000	£14,000
APR	3.4%	9.9%
Loan	14,000	14,000
Interest	724	2,128
Total loan repayment	**£14,724**	**£16,128**
Repayment period	36 mths	36 mths
Monthly repayment – interest	£20	£59
Monthly repayment – loan	£389	£389
Monthly repayment – total	£409	£448
Annual repayment – total	**£4,908**	**£5,376**

Operational costs

You have identified the following expenses:

● **Fixed costs** will not vary with the number of classes or students planned.

Table 7.2: Case Study 1: Fixed costs

	£
Class assistant's salary	16,200
Social insurance costs (employer contribution)	1,620
Pension costs (employer contribution)	480
Teaching materials	500
Costumes and uniform	300
Class props	200
Subscriptions and journals	200
Travel costs	700
Accountancy	400
Insurance	450
Telephone – fixed line and broadband	400
Systems software subscription and fees	800
Affiliation subscription and training courses	500
Office costs (home)	600
Loan interest APR 9.9% 12 × £59 (see note below)	708
Miscellaneous	600
Total fixed costs	**£24,658**

Accounting convention requires that only the interest on the loan is regarded as a fixed business expense, the capital element of the loan is required to be paid *out of* profits rather than be included as an expense *against* profits.

● **Semi-fixed costs** may vary according to the number of classes, students, or circumstances.

Table 7.3: Case Study 1: Semi-fixed costs

	£
Hire of studios	25,308
(hourly rate £19 × 37 hours × 36 weeks)	
Maintenance and repair	400
Advertising, promotion and marketing	2,000
Printing, postage and stationery	500
Mobile costs and phone calls	400
Bank and credit card (cc) charges	500
Sundry expenses	392
Total semi-fixed costs	**£29,500**

Studio rental has been classified as a semi-fixed cost because the property owner requires payment for a term in advance and, therefore, this would not vary even if there were insufficient students to run a viable class.

- **Variable costs** will vary according to the number of classes, students, or circumstances.

For a dance school, variable costs would relate to your teachers and musicians. As a start-up however, you are doing the teaching and the cost of your own time can be budgeted either by including it as a notional variable cost, or as a percentage of the profit for the business. You decide to use a notional variable cost approach by calculating your time. Your variable costs can be summarised as follows:

Table 7.4: Case Study 1: Variable costs

	£
Owner-teacher cost	24,300
Administrative time	9,720
Class assistant replacement cost (employee)	6,000
Freelance musician cost	1,898
Total variable costs	**£41,918**

The various components have been calculated as follows:

○ **Owner-teacher cost:** You will teach four classes Monday to Friday and five classes on Saturday, totalling 25 hours per week. This time can be costed as:

Monday–Friday – 5 days × 4 hours	20	(a)
Saturday – 1 day × 5 hours	5	(b)
Total hours per week (a + b)	25	(c)
Number of terms	3	(d)
Number of weeks per term	12	(e)
Total hours in year (c × d × e)	900	(f)
Total owner-teacher cost – 900 hours × £27	£24,300	

 It can be good practice to include the cost of the owner in a budget as this effectively includes a freelance "replacement" cost if sickness interferes or circumstances change. The rate of £27 is an assumed median freelance rate at the time of publication.

○ **Administrative time:** You will be spending a further 10 hours a week on administrative matters although, in reality, you will probably spend more time than this. Administration can include such duties as ensuring that the timetable runs smoothly; the assistant turns up; the studios are open and closed, in good order for classes; barres and other equipment are ready for use; invoices and reminders are mailed, debts collected, parents notified of future events; and generally keeping customers happy. Mentoring parents and carers about their children or charges can take up a lot of time.

Your business is a classic example of having to wear too many hats. Taking the same £27 rate as for a teacher, the add-on cost would be 10 hours × £27 × 36 weeks = £9,720.

☀ It can be good practice to build in your administrative costs – or provide a "salary" while the business is building up – as this time is "unseen". There may come a time when the business will have to take on someone else who will be paid to do the work. This leads to more realistic costing.

○ **Employee class assistant replacement cost:** You also employ a class assistant whose duties are to register students on arrival; deal with any problems on site; ensure students leave safely; assist in the studio when needed and any other administrative tasks that might arise. The employment contract is based on 25 hours per week per term.

☀ You should budget for a replacement assistant in case the assistant falls sick. This can be prudent as the assistant is an employee, the salary a fixed cost, and entitled to sick pay.

A replacement cost has been budgeted at a rate of £18 per hour plus 10% for additional employer costs (assistants can be categorised as casual employment and subject to social insurance and pension costs).

Monday–Friday – 5 days × 4 hours	20	(a)
Saturday – 1 day × 5 hours	5	(b)
Total hours per week (a + b)	25	(c)
Number of weeks per term	12	(d)
Total hours in year (c × d)	300	(e)
Class assistant replacement cost – 300 hours × £20[2]	£6,000	

---

[2] Includes 10% additional cost on the hourly rate of £18

Budget for at least one term's costs as it can be easier to recruit a replacement for a longer period.

- **Freelance musician cost:** You will provide live accompaniment in class for one week per term with each class covered by a musician. Their time has been budgeted at £23 per hour plus 10% in additional employer costs (musicians can be categorised as casual employment and subject to social insurance and pension costs).

Monday–Friday – 5 days × 4 hours	20	(a)
Saturday – 1 day × 5 hours	5	(b)
Total hours (a + b)	25	(c)
Number of terms	3	(d)
Number of weeks per term	1	(e)
Total hours in year (c × d × e)	75	(f)
Total freelance musician cost – 75 hours × £25.30[3]	£1,897.50	

Providing 25 hours of continuous work in a single week can be attractive to a freelance musician.

You have now calculated the fixed, semi-fixed and variable costs. Your budgeted costs total £96,076:

Table 7.5: Case Study 1: Summary of costs

	£
Fixed costs	24,658
Semi-fixed costs	29,500
Variable costs	41,918
Total costs	**£96,076**

Owner earnings and profit

Having included all the business costs in the budget, you need to be sure that you can earn a reasonable living from your business, repay the start-up loan and any other funding identified. You need to add a profit element (the *cost plus* approach) to the budget to provide a salary for your living expenses, tax, pension, borrowings and other necessities. The profit element can differ from industry to industry but as cost is being used to determine fees, it makes sense to look at your needs to determine the profit element.

[3] Includes 10% additional cost on the hourly rate of £23

List all your living and personal expenditure to arrive at the level of income you want from your business. Be realistic.

Let us assume you calculate a need for an income of £29,656 (£25,000 for your personal needs and £4,656 to repay the loan for the next three years). As discussed earlier, you decided to use a notional variable cost approach by calculating and including your time in the costs. Your needs of £29,656 are more than adequately covered by this approach – £34,020 (£24,300 teaching cost and £9,720 administrative time):

	£
Your teaching time	24,300
Your administrative time	9,720
Your "salary"	**£34,020**

However, this costing also leaves little margin of error if circumstances change through sickness or family considerations and the business has to employ a teacher and an administrator to replace you.

Adding a further £29,656 (approximately 31% profit) to the budgeted costs would require your dance school to generate total revenues of £125,732, assuming you meet the number of classes and the number of students. Based on the number of hours (900) and achieving 15 students per class, this would result in an hourly class fee of £9.31 per student:

$$£125,732 \div 900 \div 15 = £9.31$$

However, you are concerned that £9.31 might be too high, as you may have to charge value added tax.

Although some of the notional costs were built in to provide a buffer for sickness, unexpected expenditure and future reserves, you are confident that at the beginning of your career you are fit and healthy. You are, therefore, prepared to take the risk that these costs will not be used in their entirety, and are willing to reduce the profit to £10,000 (approximately 10% × £96,070) plus the annual loan capital of £4,656.

 Many start-ups assume they are fit, healthy and enthusiastic to bring the Business Plan to fruition.

This would mean that your profit, after the loan repayment, could be potentially £44,020:

Table 7.6: Case Study 1: Earnings and profit

	£
Your teaching time	24,300
Your administrative time	9,720
Your profit	10,000
Earnings (salary) and profit	**£44,020**

This profit would be more than sufficient to cover your personal needs of £25,000 and to create a buffer of £19,020 between £25,000 and £44,020.

There is also a further cushion of £6,000 for a replacement assistant, which may not be used. This may appear excessive but it is building in future shock and providing a buffer not only in case of sickness, but also a shortfall in students, or higher than expected costs in the initial years. (Refer to *Chapter 9: Analysing Cash Flow.*)

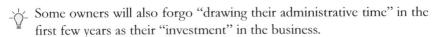 Some owners will also forgo "drawing their administrative time" in the first few years as their "investment" in the business.

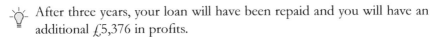 After three years, your loan will have been repaid and you will have an additional £5,376 in profits.

Budgeted income and expenditure

XYZDanz needs to generate total revenue of £110,732:

	£
Costs	96,076
Profit	10,000
Loan repayment	4,656
Total revenue required	**£110,732**

The revenue may or may not be subject to value added or sales tax, depending on the threshold for consumption taxes in the country in which the business is set up. In the United Kingdom, *e.g.,* this level of revenue would be subject to value added tax but a taxpayer may be able to take advantage of an exemption available under VAT Tribunal case law. (Refer to *Chapter 11: Paying Taxes* in the section on Consumption Tax.)

Inserting the revenue required, *XYZDanz*'s budget would look like this:

Table 7.7: Case Study 1: Budgeted income and expenditure

	£	£
Total revenue (fees)		£110,732
Owner-teacher cost	24,300	
Administrative costs	9,720	
Class assistant replacement costs	6,000	
Freelance musician costs	1,898	
Variable costs		41,918
Hire of studios	25,308	
Maintenance and repair	400	
Advertising, promotion and marketing	2,000	
Printing, postage and stationery	500	
Mobile costs and phone calls	400	
Bank and credit card (cc) charges	500	
Sundry expenses	392	
Semi-fixed costs		29,500
Class assistant's salary	16,200	
Social security costs (employer contribution)	1,620	
Pension costs (employer contribution)	480	
Teaching materials	500	
Costumes and clothes	300	
Class props	200	
Subscriptions and journals	200	
Travel costs	700	
Accountancy	400	
Insurance	450	
Fixed line and broadband	400	
Software subscription and fees	800	
Affiliation subscription and training courses	500	
Home office costs	600	
Loan interest APR 9.9% 12 × £59	708	
Miscellaneous	600	
Fixed costs		24,658
Total expenditure		96,076
Net profit		**£14,656**

If space and resources are available, additional income can be generated by activities such as:

- Seasonal dance weeks/fortnights (often known as summer or Easter schools) and school shows during holiday periods.

- Fitness or adult learning classes running alongside regular classes.

- Some activities can result in losses if sales are not achieved or costs are too high, but can be seen as a marketing exercise.

Breaking-even

As the old adage goes "turnover is vanity, profit is sanity, cash is a reality", break-even can be used to determine the point at which sufficient cash is being generated. The break-even point (BEP) – the point at which you start to make money, where costs equal income – can be calculated once you have completed your budget.

The BEP is where the business is not making any profit, but costs are covered. Any excess income over the BEP will be profit, while any shortfall will be a loss.

XYZDanz's budgeted profile is:

Table 7.8: Case Study 1: Budgeted profile

	£
Fixed and semi-fixed costs	54,158
Variable costs	7,898
Owner-teacher admin time	34,020
Profit element	14,656
Total revenue (fees)	**£110,732**

Break-even by gross profit margin

Using gross profit margin, your annual BEP will be achieved with sales of £58,297:

- Gross profit = sales – variable cost

  Gross profit % margin = gross profit ÷ sales × 100

  Break-even point by sales = (fixed and semi-fixed costs ÷ gross profit % margin) ×100

- Gross profit = (£110,732 – £7,898) = £102,834

Gross profit % margin = £102,834 ÷ £110,732 × 100 = 92.9%
Break-even point = £54,158 ÷ 92.9% × 100 = **£58,297**

Break-even by revenue per school term or per week

You can refine this by expressing it by the number of terms or school weeks in a year:

○ Break-even point per term = £58,297 ÷ 3 = £19,432
○ Break-even point per week = £58,297 ÷ 36 = £1,619

Break-even by unit

Alternatively, you could express the BEP in classes or students, or costs/revenue by using the other equations.

○ Break-even point in units = fixed cost ÷ (sales price − variable cost).
○ Break-even point in costs/revenue = the break-even point in units × sales price.

Using *XYZDanz*'s profile:

○ Financial profile (per hour):

	£	Hours	£ per hour
Fixed costs	24,658	900	27.40
Semi-fixed costs	29,500	900	32.77
Variable costs	7,898	900	8.78
Owner-teacher admin time	34,020	900	37.80
Profit element	14,656	900	16.28
Total revenue	**£110,732**	**900**	**£123.04**

○ Attendance profile (per week):

Number of classes per week	25	
Number of weeks per term	12	
Number of classes per term	300	(a)
Average number per class	15	
Number of students per week[4]	375	(b)

[4] Pupil roll can include the same pupil taking more than one class

○ Fixed and semi-fixed cost profile (per term):

Fixed costs	£24,658	
Semi-fixed	£29,500	
Total fixed and semi-fixed costs	£54,158	
Per term (÷ 3)	£18,053	(c)

○ Fees per class and per student (per term):

Total fees received (3 terms)	£110,732	
Fees per term	£36,911	(d)
Budgeted number of classes per term (a)	300	
Average fee per class per term (d) ÷ (a)	£123.04	(e)
Budgeted number of students per term (b)	375	
Average fee per student per term (d) ÷ (b)	£98.44	(f)

○ Variable costs per class and per student (per term):

Variable costs (3 terms) (excluding notional costs)	£7,898	
Variable costs per term	£2,633	(g)
Budgeted number of classes per term (a)	300	
Variable cost per class per term (g) ÷ (a)	£8.78	(h)
Budgeted number of students per term (b)	375	
Variable cost per student per term (g) ÷ (b)	£7.02	(i)

Using the formulae, and adjusting them to the business, the relative units can be both per class and per student:

○ Per class

Break-even point per class (units) = fixed cost ÷ (sales price – variable cost)

Break-even point per class (units) =   (c)   ÷ ((e)   –   (h)   )

Break-even point per class = £18,053 ÷ £114.26 (£123.04 – £8.78)

Break-even point per class = **158 classes**

○ Per student

Break-even point per student (units) = fixed cost ÷ (sales price – variable cost)

Break-even point per student (units) =   (c)   ÷ ((f)   –   (i)   )

Break-even point per student = £18,053 ÷ £91.42 (£98.44 – £7.02)

Break-even point per student = **197 students**

Break-even by unit revenue per class or per student

Using the number of classes or the number of students, the BEP can also be expressed by class or student revenue per term:

Break-even point in costs/revenue = the BEP in units × sales price
Break-even point in revenue = the BEP per class × sales price

Break-even point by class revenue = 158 × £123.04 = £19,440 per term
Break-even point by student revenue = 197 × £98.44 = £19,393 per term

The BEP illustrates the number of classes (with 15 in each class or averaged across all classes) that you need to hold, or the number of students that you need to attract to cover your fixed and semi-fixed costs.

The BEP represents 53% of your budget. Any additional students or classes will start to generate an income for you.

 When determining the BEP, keep in mind that it is not a magic number. It is a best-guess point that provides insight into how cash and profit (and loss) changes as sales go up and down, or if there is a change in the mix of costs. In *XYZDanz*'s case, the unit can be the number of classes (as you could base your business on a full range of classes), or equally it could be the number of students if there is good enrolment across all classes.

In the next chapter, you can find out how to calculate your fees using the budget.

CHAPTER 8

SETTING FEES

KEY POINTS

Class fees: By the hour, by mix, by degree of complexity Consumption tax Reasonableness
Other fees: Private lessons and studio rental, summer schools and workshops, merchandise
External examinations: managing these costs, acting as agents

---

Chapter 2 highlighted the difficulty in business planning in determining the sales volume, and the previous chapter demonstrated the use of a *cost plus* approach to determine the required sales volume to cover business costs and personal needs.

A drawback to the *cost plus* approach is if prices are fixed too low because costs and needs are low. This has the same effect as under-pricing. It is crucial that any business calculate the correct fees or pricing to charge per unit of output. Always bear in mind that the examples and exercises in this book are illustrative only.

The main unit of output for a dance school will be the cost of attending class for a term or academic year. For other business such as a dance theatre, it will be the seat cost over the length of the production; a dance conference, the cost of attending individual or a series of workshops; or a course provider, the cost of attending the event.

This chapter looks at a number of approaches to setting fees for dance classes and other dance-associated fees. The principles can be applied to other products and services.

Class fees

There are a number of different approaches to setting class fees, such as:

● By the hour
● By mix (volume or genre)
● By degree of complexity

By the hour

Taking the cost per hour of £123.04 from the financial profile in Case Study 1 and the budgeted attendance of 15 students per class, the fee per class (before any consumption taxes) would be calculated at £8.20 per hour or £2.05 per quarter hour:

	Per hour	Per ¼ hour
Cost	£123.04	£30.76
Number of students per class	15	15
Cost per hour per student	£8.20	£2.05

Although the teaching period is 4 hours on Monday to Friday and 5 hours on Saturday, each class can be of a different duration and, therefore, it would be inappropriate to charge each class £8.20. Let us assume the actual time is set out below, and applying fees based on a rate of £2.05 per ¼ hour, the fee charged per class would change to those in Table 8.1:

Table 8.1: Calculation of hourly rates

	Total hours per week	Per class	Weekly fee income
Average hourly rate		£8.20	
6 classes of 45 mins	4½	£6.15	£553.50
13 classes of 1 hour	13	£8.20	£1,599.00
6 classes of 1¼ hours	7½	£10.25	£922.50
	25		£3,075.00
36 weeks	900 hours		£110,700

 If these fees attracted a consumption tax, you would need to add the percentage (%) tax element.

For example, if the value added tax (VAT) rate was 20%, the fee per class would have to increase to those shown in column (a) and the term fees would be as shown in column (b):

	Class fee excluding tax	VAT 20%	(a) Class fee including tax	(b) Per term (12 weeks)
45 mins class	£6.15	1.23	£7.38	£88.56
1 hour class	£8.20	1.64	£9.84	£118.08
1 ¼ hour class	£10.25	2.05	£12.30	£147.60

Fees are generally rounded up or down to more manageable amounts per class, per term, or per year.

This may result in a reduction of income but it makes the fees more user-friendly, *e.g.*, the term fees could be rounded up or down to full integers, as shown below:

	Class fee including tax		Per term (12 weeks)
45 mins class	£88.56	Rounded down to	£88.00
1 hour class	£118.08	Rounded down to	£118.00
1 ¼ hours class	£147.60	Rounded up to	£148.00

 When considering subsequent increases, it is good practice to deduct any tax from a fee first, calculate the percentage increase and then add the tax back. If you calculate a percentage increase on the tax inclusive fee, you are "profiting" the tax collector.

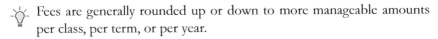 Always have a notice in your terms and conditions stating that the business reserves the right to increase fees during a school year if there is an increase in value added (or equivalent consumption) tax; otherwise the school may find that it is more difficult to pass on any tax increases until the start of a new academic year.

By mix (volume or genre)

This is a variation of the "per hour" basis. Case Study 1 assumed an average of 15 students per class, and based on the hourly rate pro rata, weekly revenue would be £3,075:

	Total hours per week	Per class	Weekly fee income
6 classes of 45 mins	4½	£6.15	£553.50
13 classes of 1 hour	13	£8.20	£1,599.00
6 classes of 1¼ hours	7½	£10.25	£922.50
	25 hours		£3,075.00

In reality, however, the attendance mix will turn out differently because of the complexity of the classes and/or the age of the students. *E.g.*, classes for younger people tend to attract greater numbers up to the age of 10 or 11, but after this age student numbers can reduce due to the competing demands of full-time education and other interests.

This will result in bigger classes at the younger age level and smaller at the older age level. Let us assume, therefore, your classes are of the following levels, age mix and attendance and priced by the hour or pro rata:

Table 8.2: Calculation of revenue by mix using hourly rates

	Level	Age	Attendance per class	Per class	Weekly fee income
2 classes of 45 mins	Pre-School	3–4	20	£6.15	£246.00
2 classes of 45 mins	Pre-Primary	5	20	£6.15	£246.00
2 classes of 45 mins	Primary	6	15	£6.15	£184.50
2 classes of 1 hour	Level 1	7	17	£8.20	£278.80
2 classes of 1 hour	Level 2	8	15	£8.20	£246.00
2 classes of 1 hour	Level 3	9	15	£8.20	£246.00
2 classes of 1 hour	Level 4	10	12	£8.20	£196.80
2 classes of 1 hour	Level 5	11	12	£8.20	£196.80
2 classes of 1¼ hours	Level 6	13	12	£10.25	£246.00
2 classes of 1¼ hours	Level 7	15	10	£10.25	£205.00
2 classes of 1¼ hours	Level 8	17	10	£10.25	£205.00
3 classes of 1 hour (Beginner, Intermediate, Advanced)	Adult		12	£8.20	£295.20
					£2,792.10

The change in attendance mix based on age and complexity will result in a lower weekly fee income decreasing from a budgeted £3,075.00 to £2,792.10, a loss of income of **£282.90** per term or £848.70 per year.

Budgeted attendance will decrease from 375 to 352, as shown below.

This changes the average attendance to 14 (352 ÷ 25). This may be a relatively small change but it is at the expense of higher attendance at the younger age end (20) which are shorter classes and cost less, than the young adult end (10) where the classes are longer, more expensive, and compete with mainstream activities.

In our example, the shortfall is only £0.80p per student (**£282.90** ÷ 352 students) but it could be greater. This income shortfall can be tackled by levelling out the individual fees, up or down.

Level	No. of classes	No. attending	Total register
Pre-School	2	20	40
Pre-Primary	2	20	40
Primary	2	15	30
Level 1	2	17	34
Level 2	2	15	30
Level 3	2	15	30
Level 4	2	12	24
Level 5	2	12	24
Level 6	2	12	24
Level 7	2	10	20
Level 8	2	10	20
Adult	3	12	36
	25		352

(a) If all the fees were levelled up, there would be a small gain of $+£1$:

	Class fee excluding tax	Change to	No. of students	Additional weekly income
45 mins class	£6.15	£7.00	110	£93.50
1 hour class	£8.20	£9.00	178	£142.40
1¼ hours class	£10.25	£11.00	64	£48.00
			352	£283.90

(b) If two of the fees were levelled up, and one down, there would be a small shortfall of $-£8$:

	Class fee excluding tax	Change to	No. of students	Additional weekly income
45 mins class	£6.15	£7.50	110	£148.50
1 hour class	£8.20	£9.00	178	£142.40
1¼ hours class	£10.25	£10.00	64	£(16.00)
			352	£274.90

🔆 The disadvantage of this method is that over time the relationship of cost to time becomes distorted.

The average hourly class fee of £8.20 equates to an average fee of 13.67p per minute. Using the fees in (a) and (b) above, the average fee per minute would be changed to between 14.67p and 15.56p per minute for (a) and between 13.33p and 16.67p per minute for (b):

		(a) Levelled fees	Fee per minute	(b) Levelled fees	Fee per minute
All classes fee	£8.20		13.67p		13.67p
45 mins class	£6.15	£7.00	15.56p	£7.50	16.67p
1 hour class	£8.20	£9.00	15.00p	£9.00	15.00p
1¼ hours class	£10.25	£11.00	14.67p	£10.00	13.33p

By degree of complexity

A third option is to re-set the fee by complexity, irrespective of time. This can be accomplished by having a banded fee for each level, as shown in Table 8.3:

Table 8.3: Calculation of revenue using banded rates

No of classes	Level	No. attending per class	Banded fee £	Weekly fee income	Fee per minute
2	Pre-School	20	£6.50	260	14.44p
2	Pre-Primary	20	£7.00	280	15.56p
2	Primary	15	£7.50	225	16.67p
2	Level 1	17	£8.00	272	13.33p
2	Level 2	15	£8.50	255	14.17p
2	Level 3	15	£9.00	270	15.00p
2	Level 4	12	£9.50	228	15.83p
2	Level 5	12	£10.00	240	16.67p
2	Level 6	12	£10.50	252	14.00p
2	Level 7	10	£11.00	220	14.67p
2	Level 8	10	£11.50	230	15.33p
3	Adult	12	£9.50	342	15.83p
				£3,074	

The change in fees to one based on complexity can result in meeting your budgeted weekly income of £3,075, but this method, as with the "by mix method", also leads to a distortion of the relationship of cost to time.

One way to avoid having to level fees is to choose an average attendance per class that is achievable for all classes. Our hypothetical mix suggests that 13 or 14 might have been a better choice than 15. This would result in a higher standard fee per hour to achieve the same financial result as 15, but would avoid having to level out fees or change according to complexity.

Consumption tax

With revenues of £110,732, *XYZDanz* may or may not be subject to value added or sales tax, depending on the threshold for consumption taxes in the country in which the business is set up. In the United Kingdom, *e.g.*, this level of revenue would be subject to value added tax but the potential owner may be able to take advantage of the exemption available under VAT Tribunal case law. (Refer to *Chapter 11: Paying Taxes* in the section on Consumption Tax.)

If a value added tax of 20% were added, the fees (by complexity) would become:

Table 8.4: Fees with consumption tax added

Level	Class fee excluding tax	VAT 20%	Class fee including tax	Per term (12 weeks)
Pre-School	£6.50	£1.30	£7.80	£93.60
Pre-Primary	£7.00	£1.40	£8.40	£100.80
Primary	£7.50	£1.50	£9.00	£108.00
Level 1	£8.00	£1.60	£9.60	£115.20
Level 2	£8.50	£1.70	£10.20	£122.40
Level 3	£9.00	£1.80	£10.80	£129.60
Level 4/Adult	£9.50	£1.90	£11.40	£136.80
Level 5	£10.00	£2.00	£12.00	£144.00
Level 6	£10.50	£2.10	£12.60	£151.20
Level 7	£11.00	£2.20	£13.20	£158.40
Level 8	£11.50	£2.30	£13.80	£165.60

Reasonableness

In terms of affordability, you should look at how the fees calculated compare with your competitors. Are they equivalent, too low or too high? Ask yourself what potential payees, parents or carers can afford? Will you attract sufficient students?

 Higher prices can be associated with a better product or service.

 Dance school fees can be less price-sensitive if the benefits of dance are understood and appreciated by the customer.

In terms of your ability to run a new school, you will need to ask yourself:

- ✓ Whether to start with fewer classes and increase gradually?
- ✓ Whether to start with more classes and spread the fixed costs?
- ✓ How many classes per week should be recommended?
- ✓ What are the grounds for the recommendation?
- ✓ Can you deliver on non-price benefits such as quality, reliability, customer care?

Other fees

Many dance schools run other activities for which an additional fee is required to participate. These activities can range from private lessons, studio rental, summer schools, workshops and merchandise to external examinations.

There are different approaches to costing fees for these activities. If the activities occur during term time, many of them can be costed by including only the variable costs and an element of profit, as semi-fixed and fixed costs would have been recovered through your class fees.

Private lessons and studio rental

As an add-on activity, private lessons normally involve a single teacher, a student and the venue. Costing can be broken down to a per hour basis. Taking figures from Case Study 1, a private lesson fee and studio rental fee can be calculated. Table 8.5 assumes that you have to rent additional space and find a teacher.

Like most one-to-one tuition, parents and carers should anticipate that a private lesson could be expensive. Private lessons could be offered to a group of 2, providing a smaller class size with the intimacy of one-to-one, but halving the overall cost.

Depending on availability, studios could be rented to students for their own practice, as well as community groups for meetings and other hirers.

Table 8.5: Calculation of private lesson and studio rental rates

	Private lesson	Studio rental	
	£	£	
Cost of venue per hour	20.00	20.00	Includes light and heat
Cost of teacher	27.00	–	Hourly freelance rate
Overtime for assistant	20.00	20.00	Assumes premises have to be kept open
Profit element	8.00	8.00	12% profit on £40
	75.00	48.00	
VAT @ 20%	15.00	9.60	
	£90.00	**£57.60**	

 Ensure that you and your hirers are properly insured and aware of their respective responsibilities for risk assessment, health and safety and music licensing.

 Ensure that all your costs are included when you set a fee to be charged.

Summer schools and workshops

As Case Study 1 assumed you only rented the studio for 36 weeks, you could take the opportunity to rent the studios outside your term times, or plan a summer school at another venue offering dance activities to the community for one or two weeks, perhaps bringing in guest teachers. These activities would need to be budgeted separately, but following the same principles set out in earlier chapters.

Merchandise

Costing merchandise is a function of the price you obtain from your suppliers. The selling price for each product should be built up from the pre-tax purchase price, delivery cost, storage cost, handling cost, desired profit, and any value added or consumption tax. The storage cost and the cost of having money tied up in merchandise should not be overlooked.

If you wish to sell merchandise, consider stock levels, sizes, colours and brand as well as the size of the investment, stocking costs and insurance. Mistakes can be costly and can lead to write-offs due to obsolete or slow-moving stock. Pre-orders from customers can mitigate over-ordering.

External examinations[1]

Some schools offer external examinations as a means of benchmarking the progress of the students. There will be costs associated with these examinations for the candidates, parents or carers:

○ The Dance Awarding Organisation will charge an examination fee for each candidate.

○ The school may require students to take additional classes to ensure the student is at the standard required for the exam.

For the school, this can involve additional costs such as hiring more studio time, additional administrative help for the extra classes and, during the examination perhaps an examination assistant, provision of refreshments for the examiner, etc.

These costs will be passed on to candidates, parents or carers and, in addition, there may be a requirement for candidates to wear an examination uniform, which is a further cost for the candidates, parents or carers.

● **Managing these costs**

A public or state sector school might normally absorb the costs of delivering private sector examinations, particularly the fee charged by an external examination board. In the private sector, these costs are usually borne by the candidates, parents or carers.

Charging separately for any additional coaching costs, including the cost of the examination day, can stretch personal budgets of payees who also have to pay the examination fee as well as uniform cost.

For example, using the fees from Table 8.4, a Level 3 class costs £10.80 a class, £129.60 a term (12 weeks), or £388.80 a year (36 weeks). When a student is ready for an examination, the school might suggest that the student takes five additional classes at £10.80 a class, and charge an administration fee of £12 for the day of the examination. This would cost the parent, carer or student an additional £66:

(£9 per class × 5 + admin fee £10) = £55 + 20% VAT = £66

The options open to the business are:

✓ Charging the payee an additional £66 in addition to the examination fee

✓ Absorbing these costs into the school fee structure

[1] (Royal Academy of Dance, 2015)

Instead of charging the payee for the additional coaching costs, the £55 (£66 with VAT) could be added into the annual cost of attending classes. The regular class fee would have to increase by £1.53 per class (£1.83 with VAT):

$$£55 \div 36 \text{ weeks} = £1.53 + 20\% \text{ VAT} = £1.83$$

If this method was adopted, the school would have to assume that over a school year all the students would be entered for an examination. If only half the school took exams each year, then the increase could be reduced by 50%. It would still need to be applied to all class fees, as it would be virtually impossible to determine who was going to take an exam. This would enable the business to recoup the cost of the additional coaching without having to charge for it separately, and the overall increase is relatively small.

☀ You could state "your fees include coaching for examinations" as one of your Unique Selling Propositions (USPs).

You could extend this to "your fees include coaching and examination fees", by calculating an average examination fee and adding this to the cost of class during the year. Not knowing how many students might take an examination and the implications of value added tax presents the same difficulty in this method as before. The number of students taking examinations each year would have to be consistent year on year for this method to work.

Example

Assuming that exams are only available between the Primary level and Level 8, you have budgeted for a class mix of 236 students. If 100% of these students, as shown in Table 8.6 column (a), took an exam during the school year, the average fee would work out at £45.72, as shown in column (c).

If a smaller number took exams but in the same proportional mix, the average would be the same, but if the proportional mix changed, as shown in column (b), the average fee would also change to £42.70, as shown in column (d).

If you took the £55 cost of the additional coaching and £46 as the average fee for examinations, the cost per class for Primary to Level 8 would have to increase by £2.80 per class (£3.36 with VAT):

$$£55 + £46 = £101 \div 36 \text{ weeks} = £2.80 + 20\% \text{ VAT} = £3.36$$

Table 8.6: Calculation of inclusive external examination fee

(a) Class size	(b) Taking exams		Exam fee £	(c) Fees £	(d) Fees £
30	30	Primary	37	1,110	1,110
34	34	Level 1	38	1,292	1,292
30	20	Level 2	40	1,200	800
30	10	Level 3	46	1,380	460
24	10	Level 4	48	1,152	480
24	10	Level 5	50	1,200	500
24	10	Level 6	54	1,296	540
20	5	Level 7	54	1,080	270
20	5	Level 8	54	1,080	270
236	134			£10,790	£5,722
Average exam fee				**£45.72**	**£42.70**

This will work if 100% of your students take exams at least once a year. Similar problems arise as with absorbing the coaching fees if less than 100% of the students take an exam or the mix is not proportionate. If the number of candidates more realistically represented column (b) (134 candidates or 56% of the total students) and you used the lower average exam fee, you would need to be sure that the number and mix of candidates was consistent year on year.

Businesses need to seek appropriate professional advice on the tax implications (and the impact on the calculation of thresholds) where dance schools either incorporate examination fees or add their own costs to the examination fees charged by a Dance Awarding Organisation.

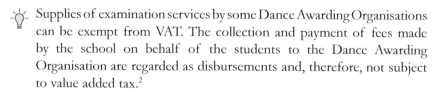 Supplies of examination services by some Dance Awarding Organisations can be exempt from VAT. The collection and payment of fees made by the school on behalf of the students to the Dance Awarding Organisation are regarded as disbursements and, therefore, not subject to value added tax.[2]

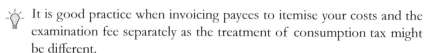 It is good practice when invoicing payees to itemise your costs and the examination fee separately as the treatment of consumption tax might be different.

[2] (HM Customs and Excise, 2018)

Amalgamating the two into a single fee might alter the tax-exempt nature of the examination fee.

 Incorporating the cost of an exempt examination fee into regular fees can inflate the overall cost to the payee if the dance school was subject to value added tax as the combined fee would be subject to VAT.

If you decided to absorb examination costs, your budget would have to be amended as appropriate.

● **Acting as an agent**

If your dance school decides to offer external examinations to your students, there are generally two sets of relationships:

The business has contracted a Dance Awarding Organisation to provide an examination service for a certain cost – the examination fee.

The business is acting as agent or trustee of the candidate, parent or carer for the examination fee.

 There is not usually a direct relationship between a Dance Awarding Organisation and the student, although they will have an obligation towards the successful candidate. If you collect exam fees direct from the candidate, parent or carer, it is recommended that exam fees are paid into a separate bank account, so that the obligation of the school towards the Dance Awarding Organisation can be met in case of any cash flow difficulties within your school.

 When invoicing the candidate, parent or carer for the examination you should separate your own costs from the Dance Awarding Organisation examination fee. Some businesses aggregate their costs with the entry fee, and then pass off the combined costs as the examination fee. This is misleading, incorrect and can have consumption tax implications.

Case Study 1's budget has been used to calculate break-even and set fees. In the next chapter, it will be used to create a cash flow statement.

CHAPTER 9

ANALYSING CASH FLOW

KEY POINTS

Business Plan assumptions   Income and receipts   Receipts and collection profile
Expenditure and payments   Business expenditure and payment profile
Cash flow statements   Drawings and savings profile

The income and expenditure in Case Study 1 reflected a normal teaching year operating at expected volume and costs. It described the potential profit but did not describe the behaviour of the income and expenditure, *i.e.*, the pattern of receipts and payments within a business – the cash flow.

There are many reasons a business can suffer cash flow problems, not least at the beginning because targets are not met, and costs escalate, but also because there may be a downturn in the economy, poor decision making or mismanagement, or other factors outside the control of the business.

As stated in *Chapter 6: Using Financial Tools*, any of these symptoms can indicate that a business is experiencing cash flow problems:

✓ Overdraft limit reached – credit problems

✓ Difficulty in paying salaries and wages each month

✓ Difficulty in paying suppliers on time

✓ Customers are slow to pay

✓ Behind with key payments such as premises rental

✓ Lack of working capital – surviving day-to-day

✓ Lack of profitability - insufficient funds to support your personal needs

✓ Unable to pay for professional advice

The pattern of receipts and payments will settle down as a business matures, but in the early years, it takes time to build up a loyal customer base. Cash flow analysis can be used to indicate when cash flow problems might occur and when additional funding might be needed to tide over a new business.

This chapter shows how cash flow analysis can be used in a similar way to a "What if" scenario to determine what the cash flow might be in the early years based on a number of assumptions about volumes, fees, receipts, costs, expenditure and payment. The same principles can be used for cash flow issues in future years, or determining a project's rate of return or value.

The cash flow analysis will show us the need for temporary, short-term or long-term funding.

Business Plan assumptions

The chapter on writing a Business Plan recommended that you should:

✓ Indicate how you intend to charge – per week, month, term, or walk-in (on the door)

✓ Indicate how you will collect fees – cash, mobile, web, factoring

✓ Indicate any initial projected shortfall

✓ Account for a time lag between invoicing and collection

✓ Account for regular and irregular payments, both business and personal

✓ Account for any existing business loans

✓ Account for any third party investment already agreed

✓ Include your own investment

Let us assume your specific assumptions were:

Income and receipts

● Frequency of fee invoicing

Classes invoiced per term, apart from adults who may pay class-by-class (walk-in).

● Method of fee payment

Customers will pay by credit card, debit card, internet payment or your preferred payment provider. You have stated that you will not accept cash or cheques.

● Fee and costs levels

Class fees will not be increased and you expect costs to remain static for the first three years.

● Projected income shortfall

Budgeted sales volumes will not be met until the third year. You project that you will start with 15 classes in the first year, 20 in the second year, and achieve 25 in the third year. You anticipate that you will meet your overall average of 15 students per class for each year.

☀ Break-even was calculated at 197 students. Your first year projection is based on achieving 225 students (15 classes × 15 students = 225).

☀ This is essentially a "What if" question. What (happens) if classes are phased in over a three-year period? (The period can of course be longer.)

Taking Case Study 1's average budgeted cost per class hour, you can work out the projected revenues and shortfall:

Table 9.1: Case Study 1: Cash flow income projection

		First year	Second year	Third year
No of classes per week	(a)	15	20	25
No of weeks per year	(b)	36	36	36
Total classes per year (a × b)	(c)	540	720	900
Average fee per class hour per week	(d)	£123.04	£123.04	£123.04
Total income (c × d)	(e)	£66,441	£88,588	£110,732
Budgeted income		£110,732	£110,732	£110,732
Income shortfall		£44,291	£22,144	–

In the first year, there would be a significant income shortfall, which narrows in the second and achieves target in the third.

● Timing of fee payments

Receipt profiles differ for every type of business depending on a number of factors, such as:

✓ How customers are invoiced

✓ When they are invoiced

✓ Who the payee is

✓ Terms and conditions of attendance

✓ Enforceability of those terms

✓ Methods of payment

You anticipate parents, carers or attendees will not all pay on time and your receipts profile will be as shown in Table 9.2.

The invoiced amounts are taken from the projection in Table 9.1 (line e) invoiced on a termly basis. The percentage received (%) reflects your best estimate of when your customers will pay. The peaks relate to the invoicing at the beginning of each term.

 This is another "What if" question. What (happens) if customers do not pay on time?

Table 9.2: Receipts and collection profile

	Collection %			Collection profile £		
Invoiced	Term 1	Term 2	Term 3	Year 1 £	Year 2 £	Year 3 £
Per year				£66,441	£88,588	£110,732
Per term				£22,147	£29,529	£36,911
September	50%			11,073	14,765	18,455
October	25%			5,537	7,382	9,227
November	10%			2,215	2,953	3,691
December	8%			1,772	2,362	2,953
January	5%	52%		12,624	16,832	21,039
February	2%	23%		5,537	7,382	9,228
March		12%		2,657	3,543	4,430
April		7%	55%	13,731	18,308	22,884
May		5%	25%	6,644	8,859	11,074
June		1%	11%	2,658	3,544	4,429
July			7%	1,550	2,067	2,584
August			2%	443	591	738
Inflow	100%	100%	100%	**£66,441**	**£88,588**	**£110,732**
Income shortfall				**£44,291**	**£22,144**	**–**

You assume that that your customers' % payment pattern is repeated in the second and third years with the higher income, although both attendance and the collection profile could be better or worse than you anticipate; in which case you would need to consider what action to take.

Expenditure and payments

You will pay your suppliers on time and in accordance with their terms.

 It is always worth remembering that payments are the opposite of receipts and, as a business, you would like to honour your suppliers' terms and conditions as you would expect your customers to honour yours.

You expect your business expenditure and payment profile to be as shown in Table 9.3. Expenditure is taken from Case Study 1's budget and the twelve columns to the right show when you expect to pay your suppliers.

Exclusions from the expenditure profile

You should note that the expenditure profile excludes any notional teaching and administrative costs as these are treated as your salary (see **drawings** below) from the profits, and a further £7,308:

○ £6,000 set aside as a provision for the replacement assistant cost as it has not been spent.

○ £600 claimed as the business proportion of home expenses as these will be paid from your personal expenditure.

○ £708 interest on the start-up loan as this will form part of the loan repayment and will be treated as a payment from net flows from the business.

Cash flow statements

A cash flow analysis is intended to project the funds you need to keep the business liquid.

The Receipts and collection profile (Table 9.2) and the Business expenditure and payment profile (Table 9.3) form an essential part of your cash flow analysis. They are combined to show the flows in and out of the business, *i.e.,* the net cash that your business generates from trading.

Personal investment

As self-employed, you do not receive a salary, as your earnings are the profits of the business. Any monies you actually take out of the business, such as your notional teaching and administrative time, are called **drawings**, which are monies withdrawn by the owner (or sole proprietor, or the partners) from a business against future profits.

As you will have anticipated from your plan to offer only 15 classes in your first year and 20 in your second, there will be a shortfall of income in the first and second years. This will have an impact on your ability to draw the £25,000 you calculated for your personal needs. You will need to reduce your drawings to a more manageable level. You estimate that you could live on £1,500 per month in Year 1, £1,700 per month in Year 2 and £2,000 in Year 3, and make the savings shown in Table 9.4.

Table 9.3: Business expenditure and payment profile

		Budget £	Aug £	Sep £	Oct £	Nov £	Dec £	Jan £	Feb £	Mar £	Apr £	May £	Jun £	Jul £
Musician costs	Annually	(1,898)					(1,898)							
Studio rental	Monthly	(25,308)	(2,109)	(2,109)	(2,109)	(2,109)	(2,109)	(2,109)	(2,109)	(2,109)	(2,109)	(2,109)	(2,109)	(2,109)
Maintenance	Periodic	(400)	(75)		(75)		(75)		(50)		(75)		(50)	
Advertising	Quarterly	(2,000)	(500)			(500)				(500)				(500)
Stationery	Monthly	(500)	(42)	(40)	(42)	(42)	(42)	(40)	(42)	(42)	(42)	(42)	(42)	(42)
Mobile costs	Monthly	(400)	(34)	(33)	(33)	(33)	(34)	(33)	(33)	(33)	(34)	(33)	(33)	(34)
Bank/cc charges	Monthly	(500)	(41)	(42)	(42)	(42)	(41)	(42)	(42)	(42)	(41)	(42)	(42)	(41)
Sundry expenses	Monthly	(392)	(32)	(33)	(33)	(33)	(32)	(33)	(33)	(33)	(32)	(33)	(33)	(32)
Assistant's salary	Monthly	(16,200)	(1,350)	(1,350)	(1,350)	(1,350)	(1,350)	(1,350)	(1,350)	(1,350)	(1,350)	(1,350)	(1,350)	(1,350)
Social insurance	Monthly	(1,620)	(135)	(135)	(135)	(135)	(135)	(135)	(135)	(135)	(135)	(135)	(135)	(135)
Pension	Monthly	(480)	(40)	(40)	(40)	(40)	(40)	(40)	(40)	(40)	(40)	(40)	(40)	(40)
Teaching materials	Termly	(500)	(167)				(166)				(167)			
Costumes	Termly	(300)	(100)				(100)				(100)			
Class props	Termly	(200)	(67)				(66)				(67)			
Journals	Annually	(200)					(200)							
Travel costs	Monthly	(700)	(59)	(58)	(58)	(58)	(59)	(58)	(58)	(58)	(59)	(58)	(58)	(59)
Accountancy	Half yearly	(400)						(200)						(200)
Insurance	Annually	(450)	(450)											
Telephone	Quarterly	(400)		(100)			(100)			(100)			(100)	
Software	Monthly	(800)	(66)	(67)	(67)	(67)	(66)	(67)	(67)	(66)	(67)	(67)	(67)	(66)
Affiliation/courses	Periodic	(500)	(300)			(100)				(100)				
Miscellaneous	Monthly	(600)	(50)	(50)	(50)	(50)	(50)	(50)	(50)	(50)	(50)	(50)	(50)	(50)
Outflow		(54,748)	(5,617)	(4,057)	(4,034)	(4,559)	(6,563)	(4,157)	(4,009)	(4,658)	(4,368)	(3,959)	(4,109)	(4,658)

Table 9.4: Drawings profile and savings

	Year 1 £	Year 2 £	Year 3 £
Owner-teacher cost	24,300	24,300	24,300
Assistant replacement cost	6,000	6,000	6,000
Administrative costs	9,720	9,720	9,720
Salary or notional costs	**£40,020**	**£40,020**	**£40,020**
Actual drawings	£18,000	£20,400	£24.000
Saving	**£22,020**	**£19,620**	**£16,020**

The savings will assist in improving cash flow. In addition, you will invest an initial £5,000 in the business from your savings.

A Cash Flow statement should include:

✓ Monies you have invested

✓ Trading receipts or inflows into the business

✓ Trading payments or outflows from the business

✓ Loan repayments out of the business

✓ Salary drawings by the owner

✓ Personal income tax payable

✓ Corporation tax payable (as applicable to business structure)

✓ Dividends (as applicable to business structure)

✓ Capital investment (if applicable)

No provision has been made for personal income tax on your earnings. How to calculate what tax might be due is discussed in *Chapter 11: Paying Taxes*. It is likely that in the initial years, the tax bill will be relatively small, but it will be payable out of your drawings.

The monthly cash position, combining the Receipts and Payments profiles, the Loan repayments and Drawings over the next three years is shown in the Cash Flow statements in Tables 9.5 and 9.6.

Table 9.5: Cash Flow statements Year 1 and Year 2

Year 1

		Aug £	Sep £	Oct £	Nov £	Dec £	Jan £	Feb £	Mar £	Apr £	May £	Jun £	Jul £	Total £
Receipts	(a)		11,073	5,537	2,215	1,772	12,624	5,537	2,657	13,731	6,644	2,658	1,550	65,998
Payments	(b)	(5,617)	(4,057)	(4,034)	(4,559)	(6,563)	(4,157)	(4,009)	(4,658)	(4,368)	(3,959)	(4,109)	(4,658)	(54,748)
Net inflow (outflow) before	(c)	**(5,617)**	**7,017**	**1,503**	**(2,344)**	**(4,791)**	**8,467**	**1,528**	**(2,001)**	**9,363**	**2,685**	**(1,451)**	**(3,108)**	**11,250**
Monthly loan repayments	(d)	(447)	(447)	(447)	(447)	(447)	(447)	(447)	(447)	(447)	(447)	(447)	(447)	(5,364)
Monthly drawings	(e)	(1,500)	(1,500)	(1,500)	(1,500)	(1,500)	(1,500)	(1,500)	(1,500)	(1,500)	(1,500)	(1,500)	(1,500)	(18,000)
Inflows (withdrawals)	**(f)**	**(7,564)**	**5,069**	**(444)**	**(4,291)**	**(6,738)**	**6,520**	**(419)**	**(3,948)**	**7,416**	**738**	**(3,398)**	**(5,055)**	**(12,114)**
Opening bank balance (overdrawn)	(g)	5,000	(2,564)	2,505	2,061	(2,230)	(8,968)	(2,448)	(2,867)	(6,815)	601	1,339	(2,059)	
Total cash inflow (outflow)	(f)	(7,564)	5,069	(444)	(4,291)	(6,738)	6,520	(419)	(3,948)	7,416	738	(3,398)	(5,055)	
Closing bank balance (overdrawn)	**(h)**	**(2,564)**	**2,505**	**2,061**	**(2,230)**	**(8,968)**	**(2,448)**	**(2,867)**	**(6,815)**	**601**	**1,339**	**(2,059)**	**(7,114)**	

Year 2

		Aug £	Sep £	Oct £	Nov £	Dec £	Jan £	Feb £	Mar £	Apr £	May £	Jun £	Jul £	Total £
Receipts	(a)	443	14,765	7,382	2,953	2,362	16,832	7,382	3,543	18,308	8,859	3,544	2,067	88,440
Payments	(b)	(5,617)	(4,057)	(4,034)	(4,559)	(6,563)	(4,157)	(4,009)	(4,658)	(4,368)	(3,959)	(4,109)	(4,658)	(54,748)
Net inflow (outflow) before	(c)	**(5,174)**	**10,708**	**3,348**	**(1,606)**	**(4,201)**	**12,675**	**3,373**	**(1,115)**	**13,940**	**4,900**	**(565)**	**(2,591)**	**33,692**
Monthly loan repayments	(d)	(447)	(447)	(447)	(447)	(447)	(447)	(447)	(447)	(447)	(447)	(447)	(447)	(5,364)
Monthly drawings	(e)	(1,700)	(1,700)	(1,700)	(1,700)	(1,700)	(1,700)	(1,700)	(1,700)	(1,700)	(1,700)	(1,700)	(1,700)	(20,400)
Inflows (withdrawals)	**(f)**	**(7,321)**	**8,561**	**1,201**	**(3,753)**	**(6,348)**	**10,528**	**1,226**	**(3,262)**	**11,793**	**2,753**	**(2,712)**	**(4,738)**	**7,928**
Opening bank balance (overdrawn)	(g)	(7,114)	(14,435)	(5,874)	(4,673)	(8,426)	(14,774)	(4,246)	(3,020)	(6,282)	5,511	8,264	5,552	
Total cash inflow (outflow)	(f)	(7,321)	8,561	1,201	(3,753)	(6,348)	10,528	1,226	(3,262)	11,793	2,753	(2,712)	(4,738)	
Closing bank balance (overdrawn)	**(h)**	**(14,435)**	**(5,874)**	**(4,673)**	**(8,426)**	**(14,774)**	**(4,246)**	**(3,020)**	**(6,282)**	**5,511**	**8,264**	**5,552**	**814**	

Table 9.6: Cash Flow statement Year 3

Year 3		Aug £	Sep £	Oct £	Nov £	Dec £	Jan £	Feb £	Mar £	Apr £	May £	Jun £	Jul £	Total £
Receipts	(a)	591	18,455	9,227	3,691	2,953	21,039	9,228	4,430	22,884	11,074	4,429	2,584	110,585
Payments	(b)	(5,617)	(4,057)	(4,034)	(4,559)	(6,563)	(4,157)	(4,009)	(4,658)	(4,368)	(3,959)	(4,109)	(4,658)	(54,748)
Net inflow (outflow) before	(c)	**(5,026)**	**14,398**	**5,193**	**(868)**	**(3,610)**	**16,882**	**5,219**	**(228)**	**18,516**	**7,115**	**320**	**(2,074)**	**55,837**
Monthly loan repayments	(d)	(447)	(447)	(447)	(447)	(447)	(447)	(447)	(447)	(447)	(447)	(447)	(447)	(5,364)
Monthly drawings	(e)	(2,000)	(2,000)	(2,000)	(2,000)	(2,000)	(2,000)	(2,000)	(2,000)	(2,000)	(2,000)	(2,000)	(2,000)	(24,000)
Inflows (withdrawals)	(f)	**(7,473)**	**11,951**	**2,746**	**(3,315)**	**(6,057)**	**14,435**	**2,772**	**(2,675)**	**16,069**	**4,668**	**(2,127)**	**(4,521)**	**26,473**
Opening bank balance (overdrawn)	(g)	814	(6,659)	5,292	8,038	4,723	(1,334)	13,101	15,873	13,198	29,267	33,935	31,808	
Total cash inflow (outflow)	(f)	(7,473)	11,951	2,746	(3,315)	(6,057)	14,435	2,772	(2,675)	16,069	4,668	(2,127)	(4,521)	
Closing bank balance (overdrawn)	(h)	**(6,659)**	**5,292**	**8,038**	**4,723**	**(1,334)**	**13,101**	**15,873**	**13,198**	**29,267**	**33,935**	**31,808**	**27,287**	

In the statements above:

Line "a" represents the receipts and collection profile for each of the three years. (Table 9.2)

Line "b" represents the expenditure and payments profile for each of the three years. (Table 9.3)

Line "c" represents the net cash position at the end of each month before the deduction of drawings and loan repayments. (Lines a – b)

Line "d" represents the monthly repayments for the initial start-up loan plus interest over three years.

Line "e" represents the monthly drawings, starting at £18,000 in Year 1, £20,400 in Year 2 and £24,000 in Year 3. (Table 9.4)

Line "f" represents the monthly net inflow or withdrawals. (Lines c – d – e)

Line "g" represents the opening bank balance at the beginning of each month. It assumes a starting bank balance of £5,000.

Line "h" represents the closing bank balance at the end of each month, after adding or deducting the monthly net inflow or withdrawals. (Line g ± f)

With an initial investment of £5,000, a phased start and reduced drawings in Years 1 and 2, there would be a negative cash position at the end of Year 1 that would improve by Year 2 and Year 3:

Table 9.7: Cash Flow summary Years 1, 2 and 3

	Year 1 £	Year 2 £	Year 3 £
Opening bank balance	5,000	(7,114)	814
Receipts	65,998	88,440	110,585
Payments	(54,748)	(54,748)	(54,748)
Loan repayment	(5,364)	(5,364)	(5,364)
Drawings	(18,000)	(20,400)	(24,000)
Closing bank balance	**£(7,114)**	**£814**	**£27,287**

The business however has made profits, before drawings, of £10,385 Year 1, £32,532 Year 2 and £54,676 Year 3, although the actual bank balance is overdrawn by £7,114 Year 1, but recovers to £814 Year 2 and £27,287 Year 3:

Table 9.8: Profit summary Years 1, 2 and 3

	Year 1 £	Year 2 £	Year 3 £
Income	66,441	88,588	110,732
Expenses	(54,748)	(54,748)	(54,748)
Home expenses	(600)	(600)	(600)
Loan interest	(708)	(708)	(708)
Profit	**£10,385**	**£32,532**	**£54,676**

This is a good example of the cash flow differing from profits. Table 9.9 shows how profitability is not reflected in the cash position.

Table 9.9 can be restated to show the change from your original budget. The budget projected a profit of £10,000 (after drawings and loan repayments). Your Business Plan assumed a reduction in income due to a three-year build up in classes, and the collection profile of your customers, offset by reduced personal drawings. An analysis of these changes in receipts and payments and the effect on the budget and bank balance is shown in Table 9.10.

Table 9.9: Analysis of change in Profits to Cash Years 1, 2 and 3

	Year 1 £	Year 2 £	Year 3 £
Profit	10,385	32,532	54,676
less Drawings (excluding home expenses)	(17,400)	(19,800)	(23,400)
Loan repayment (excluding interest)	(4,656)	(4,656)	(4,656)
Delay in receipts	(443)	(148)	(147)
add Opening bank balance	5,000	(7,114)	814
Closing bank balance	**£(7,114)**	**£814**	**£27,287**

Table 9.10: Analysis of change in Budget to Cash Years 1, 2 and 3

	Year 1 change £	Year 2 change £	Year 3 change £
Budgeted net profit	10,000	10,000	10,000
Reduced income	(44,291)	(22,144)	–
Delay in receipts	(443)	(148)	(147)
Savings from reduced drawings	22,020	19,620	16,020
Office home expenses	600	600	600
Net change in budget	**£(12,114)**	**£7,928**	**£26,473**
Opening bank balance	5,000	(7,114)	814
Net change in budget	(12,114)	7,928	26,473
Closing bank balance	**£(7,114)**	**£814**	**£27,287**

By calculating receipt and payment profiles and calculating cash flow over a three-year period, it is possible to see the points at which the business is projected to go into negative position, and the extent to which funding is required or savings can be made.

Understanding your cash flow helps. You can see that in each year the low points, although different in magnitude each year, coincide with the end of each term when income naturally slows down before the start of the following term. This is also indicative of a business that effectively only trades for 36 weeks a year.

As negative positions have been calculated in Year 1 and Year 2, you will need to decide how to fund these.

Even with the reduced income and reduced drawings, the business demonstrates the potential to be profitable, and therefore it might be possible to arrange a temporary overdraft facility with your bank or other forms of lending.

Alternatively, you would have to look at reducing your costs. You could save some money by reducing studio rental in Years 1 and 2 and thereby your assistant's hours as you are not using the full hours rented.

	Year 1	Year 2
Unused studio rental	£	£
10 hours per week × 36 weeks × £19	6,840	
5 hours per week × 36 weeks × £19		3,420
Reduced assistant hours		
10 hours per week × 36 weeks × £18	6,480	
5 hours per week × 36 weeks × £18		3,240
Potential savings	**£13,320**	**£6,660**

This may not be possible, and you may have to look at other ways of reducing expenditure.

Other factors than those given in this chapter can affect cash flow, and aspiring and existing businesses need to be aware of these.

The next chapter gives some ideas on the sources of funding.

CHAPTER 10

FUNDING

Starting a business requires funds, and sufficient funds to survive until the point at which income continually exceeds expenditure. These funds will enable a business to provide services to potential customers.

It is only when you have drawn up your Business Plan and prepared your income and expenditure and cash flow statements that you can know your funding requirements. As stressed in earlier chapters, assumptions and projections must be realistic, and any risks analysed. The previous cash flow examples were based on two "What if" scenarios:

✓ What (happens) if classes are phased in over a three-year period?

✓ What (happens) if customers do not pay on time?

You must remain aware that other factors might affect your start-up, such as:

✓ Demand for your services is not as buoyant as thought

✓ Fees are too high

✓ Mix of classes does not appeal

✓ Location is not convenient for customers

✓ Customers are taking longer to pay

✓ Level of bad debts is higher than expected

✓ Costs have risen

If you have a good relationship with your existing bank, they may be the best source to turn to. You may wish however to keep your personal and business banking separate. Banks offer competing products so you should check these out, and there are app-based challenger banks hot on the heels of the traditional high street banks.

Before you approach any funders, it might be worth checking out your own credit rating. This is an evaluation of the credit risk of a prospective debtor, predicting their ability to pay back a debt, based on data collected by the credit reference agency. Sometimes these agencies hold incorrect data, which can affect an ability to raise funds if not corrected.

This chapter looks at potential sources of funding.

Assessing your needs

A common rule of thumb is if your business risks are low, profits are probably relatively low too. High prices, high profits and low risk will attract competitors, consequently the market place becomes more crowded, more competitive, and profits are squeezed. Low-risk low-return businesses will find it more difficult to attract funds from investors.

Your attitude to or your appetite for risk and success will provide the answer to whether it is better to use your own money or borrow someone else's, although if the business is a high-risk venture, it might be hard to find funds. More of your own or family money helps to ensure that you are running your own business and are not dependent on anyone other than your customers and employees.

Popular reasons to borrow are to:

- ✓ Provide start-up costs
- ✓ Provide working capital
- ✓ Refurbish or purchase premises
- ✓ Invest in new equipment
- ✓ Grow a business
- ✓ Cover a one-off cost
- ✓ Hire extra staff

Finding the right lender might also depend on their appetite for risk. Some lenders are averse to risk and require collateral or guarantees; others may be more willing to lend. In most cases, it depends on how much you want to borrow. Collateral or guarantees are often derived from a borrower's net worth or access to another's net worth.

Your circumstances will differ from others. You may:

- ✓ Be starting from scratch
- ✓ Have been given an existing dance school

✓ Have been given the opportunity to buy an existing dance school

✓ Have an existing dance school that you wish to expand

In each of these cases, the calculation of what you are "worth" will be different. In simple terms: Your house, contents, car, savings, pension and insurance policies are your assets. Your personal credit cards, car payments, loans and mortgages are your liabilities. Your net worth is the difference between the two.

If you already own or have acquired a business, then you will have physical assets and the goodwill of the business name.

If you have sufficient net worth to act as collateral, the more traditional form of lending such as bank loans might be available, but if you have insufficient collateral then peer-to-peer lending or crowdfunding might be your only option.

In Case Study 1, you identified:

✓ A start-up loan of £14,000

✓ An initial personal investment of £5,000

✓ A maximum working capital cash flow shortage of £8,968 in December Year 1, £14,774 in December Year 2 and £6,659 in August Year 3

✓ All other assumptions are met

Any lender will look at your Business Plan to see if it is realistic, whether a loan and an overdraft would be a safe investment from them and whether you will be able to repay the interest and capital.

● The first consideration a lender might raise is about your initial investment. Your cash injection of £5,000 might be considered too small, and a larger amount might indicate more confidence in your Business Plan. Therefore, they might require you to use more of your personal savings (if you have any), or approach family and friends to assist. Any further funds from personal savings or family and friends would reduce the cash flow shortages identified.

● Secondly, a lender might ask whether your assumptions on phasing and class size are achievable, and whether you can live on your reduced earnings. This second consideration is to ensure that both the start-up loan and your requested working capital loan or overdraft limit will be sufficient, because a lender doesn't want you coming back a second time to request further funds, as this can create a lack of confidence. One of the criteria for success is ensuring that there is sufficient funding to cover working capital, especially when starting out.

- A third consideration might be, that while you have identified start-up costs of £14,000, the lender might question whether this is sufficient for your needs and whether an APR of 9.9% is realistic.
- A fourth consideration would be the amount of personal income tax due which would have to be paid out of your drawings, thereby reducing the amount available for your personal needs.

Sources of funds

Funding can be found through many different sources. There are both formal and informal routes.

Formal routes

Formal finance can be described as borrowing from financial institutions such as banks, credit unions and other non-financial institutions subject to regulation. Always ensure the funder you choose is regulated by the Financial Conduct Authority (FCA), the UK's independent financial regulatory body, or equivalent.

- Bank or business loan

  The most traditional source of funding is from a bank. Banks are generally the largest providers and are generally risk-averse. New businesses, without a record of accomplishment, can be considered high risk. Securing a loan requires pre-planning and preparation as well as a solid Business Plan in order to increase your chances. It can be possible to get loan drawdowns or a line of credit so that funds are only used when needed.

   There are a number of app-based challenger banks such as Monzo, Monese and Revolut, which are challenging the traditional high street banks.

- Bank overdraft

  If your bank permits it, an overdraft is the principal form of short-term funding. Overdraft limits are usually agreed after discussion by the bank, and are primarily given to cover short-term or temporary cash flow shortages. Overdrafts are usually quick to arrange and relatively cheap but restrictions and drawbacks include upper limit and instant repayment.

   In some countries, it is illegal to write a cheque that would cause an account to become overdrawn; instead, a bank or business loan would have to be taken out.

- Crowdfunding

  The most popular of this type of alternative finance is debt-based crowdfunding, also known as "peer to peer lending", "P2P", "marketplace lending", or "crowd lending".

  Peer to peer works through websites bringing together lenders and borrowers. A borrower applies online, stating the loan required, the length of the loan and the reasons why. The application is reviewed and verified by an automated system, which also determines the borrower's credit risk and interest rate.

  Borrowers repay monthly and lenders make money from the interest on the secured or unsecured loans; the system operators make money by taking a percentage of the loan and a loan-servicing fee. The website operator will administer the loan and distribute payments to the lenders.

  💡 Funding Circle, operating in the UK, US, and in some countries in Europe, is an example of a peer-to-peer lending marketplace that allows investors to lend money directly to small and medium-sized businesses.

- Technology payment platforms

  Technology companies are developing a new line of small business loans. Businesses, looking to expand or grow, with established credit patterns with companies such as Amazon, PayPal or Ant Financial, can access capital they might need. It is faster and easier than traditional loans as the companies can pre-select businesses that already process payments through them.

  💡 A PayPal working capital facility, for example, is a business loan with a fixed fee, which is repaid through an agreed percentage of sales paid through PayPal.

- Venture capital

  Venture capital is more suitable to the larger or growing business. Once established and with assets to put up as collateral for loans, you could consider selling a portion of your business to a partner or, if you have formed a company, issue shares in exchange for cash. Dilution of an owner's shareholding can result in a loss of control over the business.

- Government or fund assistance

  There can be business assistance schemes, which give access to loans, equity financing, grants and incentives. Local authorities, regional or national governments can be a source. Some funds or trusts can assist individuals who might have been out of work, or come from a particular background, *e.g.,* the armed services, young people, women, ethnic minorities.

● Credit loans

There has been a growth in high-cost short-term credit loans (HCSTC), also known as payday loans, payday advances, salary loans, payroll loans, small dollar loans, short term, or cash advance loans. These offer short-term unsecured loans with often a very high annual percentage rate (APR). These can lead to usurious terms of credit if not repaid on time.

● Credit cards (business)

You can use a business credit card to fund short-term purchases. These offer short-term unsecured loans with often a very high annual percentage rate (APR). These can also lead to usurious terms of credit if full payment is not made by the following month.

⚬ Credit card agreements do not normally allow personal credit cards to be used for business purposes.

Informal routes

Informal finance is borrowing that occurs outside the formal financial sector. It includes loans from family members, friends, rotating savings and credit associations (ROSCAs), suppliers, moneylenders ("loan sharks") and informal banks.

● Personal savings

The owners and founders of the business most commonly fund start-ups. This is the simplest approach and allows for the greatest control over your business. However, it may be several months or more before you can earn an income for yourself, so you must ensure that you have sufficient personal income for your living expenses and only use excess funds to invest in your business.

● Family and friends

You can borrow from family and friends if they are willing to invest to help you to achieve your dream. The terms may be more flexible than those offered by a bank but they should be formalised with a properly drawn up legal agreement to avoid any future misunderstandings.

● Rotating or accumulating savings and credit associations (ROSCAs and ASCAs)

These are generally found in developing countries and require an informal savings scheme to be in operation.

Funding can be obtained from a mixture of all of these sources. Both informal and formal finance have their strengths and weaknesses. Informal finance can rely more on relationships and reputation. It is good practice to meet and get to know any (bank) relationship or business development manager so that future problems can be resolved by an existing understanding of your needs and the business.

Whichever source you go to, they will want to see a detailed Business Plan and will ask for collateral or guarantees against loans.

The next chapter explains the type of earning and consumption taxes that you and your business might have to bear.

CHAPTER 11

PAYING TAXES

> **KEY POINTS**
>
> Earnings tax: income, corporate and social insurance taxes   Consumption tax: value added tax, sales tax, other taxes   Determining net profit and taxable profit   Allowable and disallowable expenses, use of home, personal use   Registration as a taxpayer and for value added and sales tax

Governments rely on individuals and companies to contribute by paying taxes. These can be direct or indirect taxes.

The most common direct taxes are those on Earnings, and the most common indirect taxes are those on Consumption. Direct taxes affect all taxpayers who earn a salary or make profits (subject to any De Minimis tax rules), whereas indirect taxes are discretionary and only affect those when a purchase is made. Other taxes might include forms of wealth tax such as Property and Inheritance; and property tax such as on Rental income or Stamp duty.

This chapter explores the nature of earnings and consumption taxes, and the difference between net profits and taxable net profits. It also provides an example of how to determine taxable profits. It is always helpful for an accountant to prepare your tax accounts or returns, but at the end of the day, you, as the taxpayer are responsible for paying the right amount of tax and so it can be useful to know something about taxes.

In whatever country you are setting up business, you should take the proper advice in determining your obligations to indirect taxation – VAT, sales and consumption taxes – their applicability to your business; and the applicability of tribunal cases such as that quoted in this chapter, where interpretation can depend on the definition of "ordinarily", the content of the instruction and the type of institution.

All of the points, including the ☀ in this chapter, need to be checked with an appropriate professional adviser or the local tax authorities to ensure that the suggested action is permissible. You should ensure that your advisers provide you with updates or links when tax rules change. Most tax authorities have comprehensive websites, which set these out.

Earnings tax

Most countries levy personal income tax on the earnings of individuals.

Income tax

Income tax is a tax imposed on an individual (the taxpayer) which will vary with their income. Some taxpayers may not earn sufficient income to pay tax. However if you do pay tax, view it as a positive because it means you are making a profit.

Taxable income for an employee is generally their salary (and income from any other sources).

Taxable income for the self-employed, whether a freelancer or with a business, is net profit derived from the business (gross fees less *allowable* business expenses) and income from any other sources.

- ☼ The self-employed do not earn a salary but are entitled to "drawdown" from the net income or profits of the business. The drawdown can be called "drawings".

- ☼ Governments can provide taxpayers with some tax relief on their earnings by giving each taxpayer a personal tax allowance. These can differ from country to country. *E.g.,* the first £10,000 of earnings might be tax-free.

Allowable business expenses are generally those spent "wholly and exclusively for the purposes of trade"; some expenses can be disallowed. Personal tax allowances depend on the taxpayer's status, and some countries allow deduction of certain personal or notional expenses. Personal income tax is then levied at the current rates.

Income from other sources could include gains from the sale of investments, goods or other property, interest, dividends, rentals, royalties, etc.

Income tax generally is derived from:

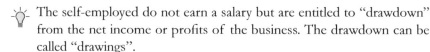

Taxable income (as computed) × (relevant) tax rate(s) = tax to pay

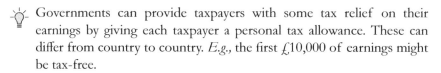

Tax rates vary widely. The tax rate may increase as taxable income increases.

If you are an employee, personal income tax will often be deducted from gross pay and collected by the employer under a withholding or pay-as-you-earn

(PAYE) tax scheme. Deductions under withholding tax schemes are not necessarily final amounts of tax, as employees may be required to disclose all income and allowances to determine actual tax at the end of each tax year. Deductions under PAYE systems are generally based on calculations by tax authorities based on information from employees, previous earnings and eligible allowances.

If you are self-employed or in a partnership, you will need to register with the relevant tax authorities. You will be required to submit income and expenditure statements on an annual basis in order to be assessed for tax purposes. This is generally called self-assessment or the equivalent. Some countries require submissions that are more frequent.

Personal income tax can be paid in arrears, in advance, quarterly, or by instalments depending on the tax jurisdiction. Late filing and late payment can incur penalties.

Corporate tax

Corporate tax, also known as company tax and corporation tax (sometimes even corporate income tax), is a tax imposed on a company (also known as the taxpayer) that will vary according to profits. This is in addition to any personal income tax that the employer (the company) may have paid on behalf of any employees under a PAYE or withholding tax scheme.

Taxable company income is usually based on the company's net profit plus or minus allowances or disallowances. The rules for computing taxable net profits will depend on the allowances a company can claim from the State, and those expenses disallowed by the State.

Net profit is defined as income less business expenses. Corporate tax is levied at the current rates on the taxable company income. Taxable income is subject to allowances and reliefs.

 A State will provide companies with tax allowances, which provide some relief on their earnings from tax. Company allowances differ from country to country. *E.g.,* tax relief on 25% of the cost of capital purchases might be an allowance.

If you are a company, you will need to register with the tax authorities and submit income and expenditure statements on an annual basis so that they can assess you for tax. This is also called self-assessment. In some countries financial statements have to be audited and may require submissions that are more frequent.

Corporate tax can be paid in arrears, in advance, or by instalments depending on the tax jurisdiction. Late filing and late payment can incur penalties. Some countries operate a system of withholding tax when paying a dividend to owners or shareholders; other countries operate a single-tier corporate tax system, which means no further tax is deducted when dividends are distributed from previously taxed income.

Social insurance tax

In addition to income and corporate taxes, countries often impose other earnings taxes on individuals and on employers. Social insurance can also be known as superannuation, national insurance, national provident or central provident. These are essentially types of income tax but can be earmarked or ring-fenced to fund retirement, pensions, benefits, unemployment, healthcare and similar outlays.

These taxes may be imposed on the employer, employee, or both, at the same or different rates.

 The self-employed can pay another rate and are not always eligible for the total range of benefits that come with these taxes.

Consumption tax

Most countries levy a type of consumption tax on goods and services. Value added tax is generally a more favoured tax among tax regimes as it avoids the cascade effect of a sales tax by only taxing the value added at each stage of production or service.

Value added tax

Value added tax (VAT), also known as a goods and services tax (GST), is a type of general consumption tax that is collected incrementally, based on the value added, at each stage of production or service.

All countries that operate a VAT system will require a business to be registered for VAT purposes. Some countries have income thresholds at which registration becomes compulsory, although in some cases it is possible to register voluntarily without reaching the threshold.

 In countries where the VAT registration threshold is quite high, there may be no advantage for a business to voluntarily register if the main costs are employee salaries, unregistered self-employed freelancers or purchases from unregistered businesses.

Unregistered businesses have to absorb the VAT on purchases from VAT-registered businesses as a business cost.

Businesses that are VAT-registered are obliged to charge VAT on goods and services that they supply to others (with some exceptions, which vary by country). They must account for the VAT to the tax authority but are entitled to offset VAT on purchases from other VAT-registered businesses, hence the incremental nature of the tax. The VAT mechanism means that the end-user tax is the same as it would be with a sales tax.

Sales tax

Sales tax is a consumer tax. It is paid by the end-user. Intermediary businesses that buy products to incorporate into their product or service generally do not have to pay a sales tax. Sales tax is collected by a business at the point of purchase by the consumer.

Other taxes

In some countries there may be two tiers of consumption tax such as in the US and Canada where there are State taxes and Provincial taxes (PST) as well as Sales taxes and GST respectively.

Other forms of consumption taxes exist such as Motor Vehicle tax, Sugar tax and Import or Customs duty.

Determining net profit and taxable profit

A business is required to keep a record of its income and expenditure. These accounting records can be used to prepare Income and Expenditure statements, Balance Sheets, Debtors, Creditors, Budgets, Cash Flow, Consumption Tax Returns and other financial statements.

From these records, the net profit of the business can be determined. Taxable income for the self-employed is the net profit derived from the business (gross fees less *allowable* business expenses).

Taxable net profit however can differ from the actual net profit because the tax authorities may consider that some business expenses should not be allowed relief against tax. Business expenses that the tax authorities recognise are called *allowable* expenses or *deductions*, and those business expenses that the tax authorities do not recognise are called *disallowable* expenses or *non-deductibles*. In addition, there may be some further allowances or reliefs relating to expenditure of a capital nature, *i.e.,* items that have a useful life that exceed one year, such as motor vehicles, pianos and other equipment. Tax authorities often allow businesses to claim a percentage of the value per annum against tax.

Effectively there are two sets of accounting records: book accounts and tax accounts (also known as tax returns).

Book accounts record the income and expenditure of the business, while the tax accounts adjust the book records for *disallowed* expenses (*non-deductibles*) and tax allowances. Accountants would normally maintain the tax accounts.

Allowable expenses[1]

The distinction between **business expenses** and **expenses allowed for tax (*allowable* expenses or *deductions*)** is that some costs can be genuine business expenses but may not be allowable as a deduction for tax relief. There may be rules relating to business expenses that disallow certain types of expenditure for tax purposes. (Refer to *disallowable* expenses or *non-deductibles* below.) This is the duality test. Generally, most business expenses are allowable and, therefore, deductible for the purposes of calculating tax if they are incurred "wholly and exclusively for the purposes of trade".

The type of costs you can claim as allowable business expenses, providing they are not for personal use, include:

- ✓ Office costs – stationery, subscriptions, journals, postage, printing, contents insurance
- ✓ Communication costs – telephone, broadband, mobile, cell
- ✓ Travel costs – fuel, servicing, repairs, motor insurance, parking, train or bus fares
- ✓ Clothing expenses – uniforms and costumes
- ✓ Employee salaries including payroll and pension costs – musicians, teachers, casual workers, administrative staff
- ✓ Freelance salaries including payroll costs – musicians, teachers, guest teachers
- ✓ Purchases – teaching materials, class props, merchandise stock sold
- ✓ Financial costs – liability insurances, bank and credit card (cc) charges, loan interest, bad debts, leasing, business credit card charges, app charges
- ✓ Occupancy costs – heating, lighting, rent, business or property rates, property insurance, repairs and maintenance, security

[1]   (HM Government, 2018)

✓ Use of home costs – see below

✓ Marketing costs – advertising, promotion, research, website costs, tradeshows, brochures, print, SEO clicks (Search Engine Optimisation)

✓ Professional fees – subscriptions, training courses, accountancy, music licences

✓ Systems – computer software, software subscription

✓ Any other costs incurred wholly and exclusively for the purposes of trade

✓ VAT would be included if the business was not registered

The rules differ from country to country, but the following type of expenditure should be allowable if:

💡 Clothing is purchased for the use of the business or for a role, such as uniforms for students or costumes for shows, and not used for any other purpose.

💡 A salary is paid at a commercial rate to a non-earning spouse, partner or other family members and related to the amount of work carried out in the business.

💡 Dance props are used solely for business purposes.

💡 Dance-related theatre and museum tickets are purchased to research into roles, styles, influences and trends; the subject is relevant and is wholly and necessary for the business.

💡 Training courses are purchased to update and enhance skills, relevant to the current business. Education would generally not be allowable *e.g.,* a degree, diploma or certificate.

💡 Pointe shoes are purchased for a performance, as they would not be practical for day-to-day wear.

💡 An insurance policy is purchased to cover a dancer's legs against injury.

💡 Bank charges and interest are incurred where a bank account is used solely for business use and not for personal expenditure as well.

Under some jurisdictions, it is possible to bring previous expenditure (from the years before trading commenced) into the business. For example, if you already owned equipment, training books, car and other resources that you intend to use in your business, these can be brought in at the value at the date the business starts.

Use of home

● **Travel**

If you have a base of operation that is distinct from your home, then the cost of travelling between home and that base would normally be treated as ordinary commuting and therefore not tax-allowable; however where the base of operation is at home the cost of travelling between home and work should be allowable.

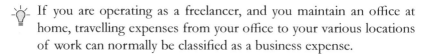 If you are operating as a freelancer, and you maintain an office at home, travelling expenses from your office to your various locations of work can normally be classified as a business expense.

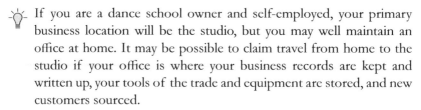 If you are a dance school owner and self-employed, your primary business location will be the studio, but you may well maintain an office at home. It may be possible to claim travel from home to the studio if your office is where your business records are kept and written up, your tools of the trade and equipment are stored, and new customers sourced.

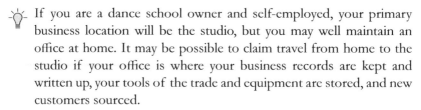 You would be able to claim travel between different school locations as a business expense.

● **Home office**

When you maintain an office at home, you will need to choose a reasonable method of apportioning costs for allowable business expenses such as heating and lighting, property tax, rent, mortgage interest, internet or telephone costs, etc. These methods could be:

○ By room: You have four rooms in your home (excluding kitchen and bathroom), one of which you use as an office. Your heating and lighting cost £800 per annum. Assuming all the rooms in your home use equal amounts of electricity, you could claim £200 as an allowable expense (£800 ÷ ¼).

○ By time worked from home: If you only work four days at home then you would have to restrict the room cost to 4/7th (£200 ÷ 4/7th = £114.28).

○ By additional cost: Before you had an office at home, your heating and lighting cost £500 a year. After you set up the office, the heating and lighting costs increased to £800. You could claim £300 as an allowable expense (the additional cost).

○ By flat rate: In the United Kingdom there is a simplified flat rate for claiming home utility bills and motor vehicle expenses.

The additional cost rule would seem the most logical while the ¼ rule or 4/7th rule could apply to expenses where the additional cost or flat rate is not appropriate.

- If you invite customers to meetings at home and provide tea, coffee, cold drinks, etc., that expenditure or a proportion of it could be classified as a business expense.

- If you use a mobile or cell phone for both personal and business, you should determine how much usage is business and how much personal; similarly, if you use the internet at home. A method could be time, if there is no individual breakdown.

If you work from home or maintain an office you need to take professional advice on whether travel is an allowable expense, what method of apportionment might be appropriate and what expense claims might expose you to future property or capital gains taxes. Exposure to these taxes can occur if you set aside an office at home for "exclusive" use rather than "sole" use. The distinction being that for the latter it can be used for other purposes when not being used as the office.

Disallowable expenses

Some costs however can be genuine **business expenses** but may be **disallowed for tax (*disallowable* expenses or *non-deductibles*)**. These expenses may have been incurred "wholly and exclusively for the purposes of trade" but fail the "duality test".

Duality is when an item can be used for a non-business purpose as well as a business purpose. Consequently, disallowable expenses are added back to net profits to arrive at the taxable net profits.

- Motor penalties such as speeding and parking tickets can be a genuine business expense, but the tax authorities do not generally allow government penalties as an allowable business expense or deduction when calculating the appropriate net profit figure for tax.

- This would apply equally to other penalties such as fines for breaking the law, filing tax returns late and penalties for the late payment of fines and taxes.

- There are often complex rules about entertainment. Some jurisdictions view (or consider) entertainment as a business expense but not as an allowable business expense or deduction. Some impose conditions stating that the entertainment needs to relate to overseas customers only, others that a majority of those attending must be non-staff. Tax authorities avoid giving tax relief for meals you would have to eat anyway.

Team meetings and lunches often fall under similar rules, but can be allowable business expenses if held away from the premises and involving travel.

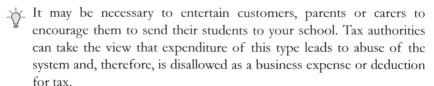 It may be necessary to entertain customers, parents or carers to encourage them to send their students to your school. Tax authorities can take the view that expenditure of this type leads to abuse of the system and, therefore, is disallowed as a business expense or deduction for tax.

- Clothes that are used for both business and non-business such as rehearsal clothes or even teaching clothes may be considered a business expense but would be disallowed as a business expense or deduction for tax.

The repayment of the capital element of a loan, *i.e.,* the amount borrowed before any interest, is generally regarded as a disallowed expense. The interest however is an allowable expense or deduction.

Personal use
Items or costs for personal use are not allowable expenses.

Many self-employed businesses include some personal expenditure within their accounts. This can be because the business pays home costs that include both business and personal usage, as do other types of cost:

- If you are using a vehicle for both business and pleasure, a reasonable method of apportioning your motor expenses such as fuel, insurance, licence, tax, repair and service costs could be the proportion of business to personal mileage. It is good practice to keep a record of mileage so that you can estimate business usage.

- Business mileage can be taken from the journey odometer or from keeping a note of post/zip codes and using an online map to calculate the mileage.

- If you mix employment and self-employment, travel to your place of employment is not a business expense, as it would be normally regarded as "ordinary commuting".

- Software used on computers for both personal and business use should be apportioned between business and personal use unless the software is entirely business-specific or the personal use is incidental.

Table 11.1: Case Study 1: Income and expenditure statement

	£	£
Total revenue (fees)		110,732
Owner-teacher cost	24,300	
Administrative costs	9,720	
Class assistant replacement cost	6,000	
Freelance musician costs	1,898	
Variable costs		41,918
Hire of studios	25,308	
Maintenance and repair	400	
Advertising, promotion and marketing	2,000	
Printing, postage and stationery	500	
Mobile costs and phone calls	400	
Bank and credit card (cc) charges	500	
Sundry expenses	392	
Semi-fixed costs		29,500
Assistant's salary	16,200	
Social security costs (employer contribution)	1,620	
Pension costs (employer contribution)	480	
Teaching materials	500	
Costumes and clothes	300	
Class props	200	
Subscriptions and journals	200	
Travel costs	700	
Accountant	400	
Insurance	450	
Fixed line and broadband	400	
Software subscription and fees	800	
Affiliation subscription and training courses	500	
Home office costs	600	
Loan repayments (£59 × 12)	708	
Miscellaneous	600	
Fixed costs		24,658
Total expenditure		96,076
Net profit		**£14,656**

Payments made to the owner of a business as drawings if self-employed, or dividends if employed, are not regarded as business expenses.

Example

Using Case Study 1 as an example to calculate the potential tax liability, a net profit of £14,656 was achieved with a turnover of £110,732 and expenses of £96,076. This is shown in Table 11.1.

The notional costs included in variable costs need to be added back to the net profit as they are regarded as **"drawings"** (against profits or earnings) and thereby disallowed. An accountant would add them back to net profit to arrive at the true net profit of the business.

Table 11.2: Net profit adjusted for drawings

	£
Net profit (Table 11.1)	14,656
Add back your salary (see below)	40,020
Adjusted net profit	**£54,676**

	£
Owner-teacher cost	24,300
Administrative costs	9,720
Class assistant replacement cost	6,000
Salary or notional costs	**£40,020**

The adjusted net profit of £54,676 in Table 11.2 represents the net profit or earnings. Let us assume the accounts include these business expenses and personal drawings, which would be disallowed for tax purposes:

- ✓ 40% of the mobile phone usage is personal
- ✓ 30% of the travel costs are personal
- ✓ No adjustment is required for the home office costs as these represent only the additional costs of the office
- ✓ Miscellaneous includes a staff lunch for £58
- ✓ Sundry expenses include a £55 parking penalty
- ✓ Drawings

The disallowable expenses identified above are added back to the adjusted net profit of £54,676 to arrive at a taxable net profit of £55,159 (Table 11.3).

Table 11.3: Taxable profits: Calculation of profit or earnings for tax

	£
Adjusted net profit	54,676
Add back disallowable expenses	
Mobile phone – personal usage 40% of £400	160
Travel costs – personal usage 30% of £700	210
Sundry expenses – staff lunch	58
Miscellaneous – penalty charge	55
Taxable profit or earnings	**£55,159**

Assuming that the *disallowable* expenses or *non-deductibles* in Table 11.3 remain the same for each of the three years, and applying these principles to the actual Net Profit in Table 9.8 from *Chapter 9: Analysing Cash Flow*, the taxable profit or earnings can be calculated for each of the years.

Table 11.4: Taxable profits Years 1, 2 and 3

	Year 1 £	Year 2 £	Year 3 £
Income	66,441	88,588	110,732
Expenses	(54,748)	(54,748)	(54,748)
	11,693	33,840	55,984
Deduct allowable personal expenses			
Home expenses	(600)	(600)	(600)
Loan interest	(708)	(708)	(708)
Profit (Table 9.8)	10,385	32,532	54,676
Add disallowable expenses or deductions			
Mobile phone – personal usage 40% of £400	160	160	160
Travel costs – personal usage 30% of £700	210	210	210
Sundry expenses – staff lunch	58	58	58
Miscellaneous – penalty charge	55	55	55
Taxable profit or earnings	**£10,868**	**£33,015**	**£55,159**

Year 3 will be the same as the calculation in Table 11.3 as this was the first year the cash flow was expected to perform on budget.

From the taxable profit or earnings, it will be possible to calculate potential tax. For example, assuming that a taxpayer is entitled to the first £10,000 of earnings as tax-free and the income tax rate was 20%, the potential income tax payable might be for each of the three years:

Table 11.5: Tax due Years 1, 2 and 3

	Taxable profit	Tax allowance	Profit adjusted for tax	Tax due
	£	£	£	£
Year 1	10,868	10,000	868	174
Year 2	33,015	10,000	23,015	4,603
Year 3	55,159	10,000	45,159	9,032

The effect of this would increase your maximum funding requirement by £174 and £4,603 respectively, but the timing of when your personal tax would be payable differs from country to country.

This is a simplistic example. There can be different rules if the business accounting year is different from the tax year. Some countries require payment by instalment, in advance or in arrears. These are all timing issues; if payment was in arrears, and you had just started up, you would not have any tax to pay until the second year, if it was by instalments or in advance, you may have to pay an estimated amount that could be too much or too little depending on how well your business performs.

Registration

As a taxpayer

When you start out in business, whether self-employed as a freelancer, a performer, a business owner, a partner or incorporated as a company, you will need to register as a taxpayer.

Depending on the country you live in, this may be as simple as an online *one-stop-suits-all* application, or one that requires completion of multiple application forms. For example:

> In the UK, if you are newly self-employed you can register online or through the HMRC helpline.
>
> In the UK, you can buy private limited companies "off the shelf".
>
> In the People's Republic of China, you need to complete a series of forms to be self-employed.

Self-employment can mean less form filling. It can be as simple as getting a tax identification number (TIN), or using an existing national identity number (NIN). A company or partnership with limited liability generally requires more detailed paperwork and fees.

Many countries issue a TIN, which is not always shown on official identity documents, while in other countries a NIN is used as a means of tracking residents for the purposes of taxation and work. This tracking can also be used for determining eligibility to receive government benefits, healthcare and other government-related functions.

In some countries, other numbers may have been introduced for a specific purpose, but over time, they have become a de facto national identification number. For example:

> In the United States, the social security number (SSN) has become almost essential to open a bank account, obtain a credit card, drive a car, etc.
>
> In the United Kingdom, there is no national identity number, and while every citizen gets a national insurance number (NINO), the self-employed require a unique taxpayer reference (UTR) number.
>
> In many European Union (EU) countries, a TIN is different from a national identity number (NIN).

A TIN is generally used for filing annual accounts, income and corporation tax. Self-employed persons are required to submit their business profits or losses and to pay tax, and this generally means that you must:

✓ Keep business records for a statutory minimum period

✓ Prepare accounts based on those business records

✓ Complete and submit a tax return, accurately reporting profits and losses

✓ Pay tax when demanded or when required to do so

✓ Inform the appropriate tax or revenue departments of any change in circumstances that may affect the tax status of the business

As referred earlier in *Chapter 5: Choosing a Business Structure*, you need to keep proper accounting records. These records make up the analysis required for preparing your accounts, and subsequently your tax returns.

For value added and sales tax

Generally, countries that have a value added tax (VAT) system or a sales tax system require businesses to be separately registered for these taxes. These registration systems normally recognise that businesses can be an individual, *i.e.,* self-employed, a sole trader (not incorporated), or a legally incorporated entity.

Countries can require businesses to register irrespective of turnover, or they can impose different thresholds or regulations specifying at which turnover level registration becomes compulsory.

Businesses that are registered for VAT or sales tax are obliged to charge VAT or sales tax (output) on the goods and services they supply to others, and account for the VAT or sales tax to the taxing authority. There may be some exceptions, which vary by country.

VAT-registered businesses, however, are entitled to offset VAT tax they pay (input tax) on the goods and services they acquire from other VAT-registered businesses. If a product or service is purchased from a business that is not VAT-registered, there is no input tax to recover.

Registration means that you have a legal duty to keep accounts for VAT and sales tax purposes. This is separate from your obligation to keep accounts for income tax purposes but, in practice, the two obligations can be met by the same set of accounting records. Registration also requires filing returns of the amount of tax collected and payment on a regular basis.

 You should register as a taxable person in the United Kingdom and any other country where your turnover or gross income per annum meets the published threshold.

 When you register for VAT, you are usually required to register in your business capacity, which would mean that if you were registering under your own name as a self-employed person, all income from whatever source – whether it be a dance school or freelance earnings – would be liable for VAT. VAT is not a selective tax; all of these would be classified as a supply of service. A company is treated as a person in VAT law.

 As stated previously, in countries where the VAT registration threshold is quite high, there may be no advantage for a business to voluntarily register if the main costs are employee salaries, unregistered self-employed freelancers or purchases from unregistered businesses.

In the United Kingdom, teachers who run their own dance schools may be able to take advantage of a VAT exemption, which states that dance teaching is as much a form of education as music, drama and aerobics.

If you comply, the exemption would apply only to your own teaching.[2] This exemption does not extend to instruction delivered by anyone employed or engaged to help. If you employed or engaged others to deliver tuition you may opt to exempt the tuition you delivered personally, but the tuition carried out by others would be treated as a taxable supply subject to any thresholds.

Tribunal Case 15201 C Clarke (deceased) and E Clarke A Clarke and H Clarke vs. Commissioners of Customs and Excise

The exemption arose out of the Tribunal case that established that under Item 2, Group 6 Schedule of the VAT Act 1994, private tuition qualifies for exemption when the supply of private tuition is in a subject *ordinarily* taught in a school or university, by an individual teacher acting independently of an employer.

The test of *ordinarily* is whether the subject is taught in a number of schools or universities on a regular basis. It had been presumed that the vast majority of structured courses delivered by an individual sole proprietor or partnership were likely to meet this criterion, but recently this exemption has not been upheld for all types of dance instruction.

For the purposes of this exemption, it is irrelevant whether the individual teacher:

- delivers the instruction to one person or to a group.
- contracts with an individual or with an organisation.
- works under a franchise agreement that allows him/her to use the teaching methods, name, or trading style of another person or organisation.

The basis for this exemption is the mandatory provision in Article 13(a) (1) (j) of the EC's Sixth VAT Directive, referring to "tuition given privately by sole proprietor or partnerships and covering school or university education".

In principle, private tuition is exempt when supplied by either a sole proprietor or any member of a partnership. Such individuals qualify as an "individual sole proprietor or partnership acting independently of an employer".

In addition to complying with tax regulations, the next chapter discusses the need for licences, permits, laws and regulations that businesses may have to comply with.

---

[2]   (HM Customs and Excise, 2018)

CHAPTER 12

UP AND RUNNING

KEY POINTS

Education   External examinations   Advertising and selling   Licensing music
Health and safety, and safe dance practice   Data protection   Other activities
Liability insurance   Public liability, abuse and molestation, product liability, professional
indemnity and employer liability   Other policies

Some types of business entity in a regulated sector or activity require appropriate licences, permits to operate.

Many countries try to keep to a minimum the number of licences and permits required, thereby reducing legislative requirements or *"reducing red tape"*. However, this is not always the case, as legislation can revolve around the type of industry, or the type of selling.

This chapter explores some issues that business owners may need to be aware of.

Education

Education can be a prescribed sector with licences and permits required.

Dance is taught in a variety of settings and sectors: universities, state schools, private dance schools, community arts/dance centres, youth and sport centres. In some settings, teachers need to achieve certain qualifications to teach in that type of institution or organisation. In some countries, irrespective of whether in the private or public sector, dance schools may need to be licensed. You should ensure that you become aware of or take professional advice and comply with any laws and regulations relating to dance in education.

It can be also important that the message and ethos of your business you communicate through your print and digital marketing is clear, as your liability to consumption taxes may be influenced by how you describe your business.

Regulatory authorities can look at websites and other public domains to obtain background information about businesses and to determine how to treat them for licensing, taxing and other regulatory issues.

External examinations

There are good reasons to consider offering formal examinations in your dance school in addition to or instead of internal assessments.

There are international Dance Awarding Organisations (DAOs) that offer qualifications in graded examinations in dance. These can be introduced to benchmark the progress of students. These examinations are usually open to adult learners, which can provide an additional USP to your business.

Dance Awarding Organisations can impose strict eligibility on who can teach and enter candidates for their examination syllabus. The eligibility criteria at its most basic might be a requirement that the teacher undertaking the physical teaching must hold a teaching qualification and membership of the Dance Awarding Organisation. Ensure that teachers you employ are compliant with any Dance Awarding Organisation regulations if you need that eligibility for your business.

These examinations are often regulated by the home country of the Dance Awarding Organisation. Some of these Dance Awarding Organisations are listed in *Appendix 4*. The international spread of these Dance Awarding Organisations provides portability of both student and teaching qualifications.

Affiliation to a Dance Awarding Organisation can be a great USP for your business. External examinations can provide a benchmark for your business as well as students. They may "anchor" the educational nature of your school, and will help students to build a portfolio of recognised achievements.

Advertising and selling

You should be familiar with laws and regulations that apply to advertising, selling and marketing practices. These are designed to protect customers from unfair or misleading trading practices and ban misleading omissions and aggressive sales tactics.

Not all of these would necessarily apply to a dance school, but you need to be aware of how you might infringe them.

○ Misleading actions might include advertising classes that do not exist, making misleading comparisons, or giving false or deceptive information about your business, status, or qualifications.

○ A misleading omission might be what has been left out rather than what is stated, such as omitting material information that a customer might need to make an informed decision about a transaction, hiding or providing material information in an unclear, unintelligible, ambiguous, or untimely manner.

> 💡 A potential example might be not informing a customer that taking an external dance examination might involve additional lessons and costs.

If you are selling merchandise there can be e-commerce regulations relating to selling over the internet.

○ In federal states such as the United States of America, the rules may differ from state to state, while in the European Union there may be implications under the VAT place of supply rules.

Licensing music

You will need licences if you copy, use recorded or live music in your business. In the United Kingdom, there are two separate collective management organisations (CMOs) called PRS for Music (Performing Rights Society) and PPL (Phonographic Performance Limited):

● PRS for Music collects money and distributes money on behalf of songwriters, composers and music publishers for the use of their musical compositions and lyrics.

● PPL collects and distributes royalties on behalf of performers and record companies for the use of their recorded music.

PRS for Music and PPL jointly offer a number of licences:

○ TheMusicLicence for playing and performing music in a business, whether through the radio, TV, other devices and/or live performances.

○ ProDub Licence for copying music to phones, tablets, iPods, CDs, laptops, MP3 players and USB keys (data storage device) for use in a business.

> 💡 If you play, perform or use music in your business you will usually need TheMusicLicence. It will cover virtually all commercially released music available.

These CMO's are authorised to sell nonexclusive licences, make reciprocal arrangements with other similar bodies, and collect royalties from these to distribute back to the owners. Other countries have their own equivalents with varying rules and regulations.

Health and safety, and safe dance practice

As a dance teacher, artist, practitioner, you will interact with the public, whether they are a young person, vulnerable adult, customer, visitor, supplier, student, teacher, examiner, parent or carer. You will have obligations of health and safety towards them when they are attending your classes, performing, taking examinations or on site.

You will also have obligations to your team, employees, freelance staff and volunteers.

Countries can require compliance with voluntary and statutory health and safety regulations and legislation.

There are also organisations which "promote and deliver best principles of safe and effective dance practice or dancer wellness to ensure a better, longer, more effective and less injured dance experience for anyone who dances, whether professionally, in competition or for recreation".

Safe in Dance International (SiDI), an organisation that works closely with international healthy dance and dance science organisations, believes that "it is the right of everyone involved in dance to teach, study, train, rehearse and perform in a safe and supportive environment. With this in mind, we support, develop, encourage and endorse the implementation of healthy dance practice worldwide." [1]

Chapter 14: Complying with the Law discusses Policies on Health and Safety in more detail.

Data protection

As a business, you will collect and hold information on your employees, freelance staff and customers through employment and payroll records, customers' details, financial records and if a dance school, student class registers, examination information, etc.

Data collection is highly regulated. Some countries have strict rules on how you might use this information and often require registration with an Information Commissioner or similar body that regulates the use of data

---

[1] (Safe in Dance International, 2018)

collected from customers; for example, consent for collecting and holding this data must be "freely given, specific and informed".

Chapter 14: Complying with the Law discusses Policies on Data Protection in more detail.

Other activities

Your dance school may be involved in other activities such as hosting school events or selling tickets for production, shows and events. These activities may be impacted by regulations such as:

○ Consumption tax levied on selling tickets to the public for an event

○ Licensing rules relating to the sale of alcohol at events

○ Permits for fundraising, holding a lottery, or soliciting donations

○ Permissions and rules relating to young persons performing in shows

○ Safeguarding regulations relating to young children and the use of photography, videoing, imagery, websites and social media

Liability insurance[2]

In addition to insuring contents, buildings and motor vehicles against fire, theft and damage, dance schools, freelancers, practitioners and artists need to consider what other insurance is required.

Liability insurance is a form of insurance for those at risk of being accused of negligence by third parties. You will recognise car insurance as the most obvious form of liability insurance – most drivers take out either third party or fully comprehensive insurance coverage.

Specialist and other forms of liability insurance, which can carry their speciality in their name, are or can be available to those who:

✓ Offer professional services to the public

✓ Offer employment

✓ Manufacture products that may be harmful

✓ Work in the construction industry

✓ Work in sport, recreation and leisure

In many countries, liability insurance is compulsory in some industries

---

[2] (Royal Academy of Dance, 2015)

because they engage in activities that can put others at risk of injury or loss. Therefore, regulation requires that such businesses should carry insurance cover to ensure that funds will be available to pay compensation in the event that business activities cause loss or damage to another. It follows that if you are uninsured and damage or loss occurs, your business could be bankrupted because you do not have the funds to cover such damage or loss.

The main Liability policies are:

Public, general or third party liability

Public liability is purchased by the insured (the first party) from an insurance company (the second party) for protection against claims made by another party (a third party). It pays damages caused to another person (a third party) where the insured is at fault.

A policy should define the insured (the first party) as not only you as the owner of the dance school but also any of your employees, freelancers and volunteers under your control.

Businesses need to consider all types of potential exposure to risk when deciding whether liability insurance is needed and, if so, how much monetary coverage is desired. Occupiers of dance premises, such as dance schools and theatres, have potentially high public liability risks because third parties frequent them. If you are renting, the property owner may assume some risks, but this should always be checked out.

A third party can include members of the public, visitors, customers, parents, carers, students, suppliers, contractors, etc. Claims can arise because of a problem with the premises or a negligent action by you and or any of your employees, such as:

- ✓ A dancer or student injured in performance or in class because of a broken dance floor
- ✓ A customer whose car is damaged by a tile falling off a roof that has not been adequately maintained
- ✓ A supplier twisting a leg on loose paving stones on your premises

"Injured" can typically include mental anguish, stress and shock. Some policies also include personal injury (*e.g.,* discrimination or defamation). Some small businesses may decide not to take out general liability insurance due to the high cost of premiums. However, in the event of a claim, out-of-pocket costs for a legal defence or settlement can far exceed the premium costs and in some cases, the costs of a claim could be enough to close down your business.

> Public liability is known as Responsabilité civile in France, Allgemeine haftpflicht in Germany, Responsabilità civile in Italy, and Responsabilidad civil in Spain

Public liability insurance can be combined with Product liability insurance (see below) and sold as Public and Product liability.

Abuse and molestation insurance

General liability policies typically cover bodily injury, and the mental anguish, stress and shock arising from the injury, but they may not cover mental and emotional harm that may form part of an allegation of abuse. You should check whether your existing liability insurance has any abuse or molestation clauses, whether the policy can be extended, or whether a separate abuse and molestation insurance policy needs to be taken out.

Abuse and molestation insurance coverage can protect businesses against a false and baseless claim of sexual misconduct, inappropriate contact by an employee, freelancer or volunteer, lack of supervision, negligence in hiring, failure to report suspicious behaviour or previous allegations and offences.

Businesses can have the most stringent vetting procedures for employees, freelancers and volunteers joining their business, but this type of unacceptable and potentially criminal behaviour cannot always be predicted or easily discovered.

This type of policy or clause goes hand-in-hand with Policies on Safeguarding young people and vulnerable adults, and Equality and Diversity, which are discussed more fully in *Chapter 14: Complying with the Law.*

Product liability

Product liability covers loss or damage suffered by someone because of a defective product—for example, a dance student who becomes injured because of a heel falling off a defective tap shoe. The complainant would have to prove it was not just wear and tear.

In such a case, a product liability claim would be made against the shoe manufacturer; however, product liability insurance is not a compulsory class of insurance in all countries. In the UK and the EU, those who manufacture or supply goods are required to carry appropriate insurance under the following laws and directives:

> UK: Consumer Protection Act 1987
>
> EU: EC Directive on Product Liability (25/7/85)

Professional indemnity

Professional indemnity insurance differs from Public liability.

> Professional indemnity insurance (PII) can also be known as
>
> Professional liability insurance (PLI), Errors & omissions (E&O) and Malpractice insurance (MI)

The teaching of dance can carry many risks. PII can protect you and your dance school against an allegation of professional misconduct, unprofessional teaching, or injury after following negligent advice.

Professional indemnity can protect against a wide range of scenarios, including:

- ✓ Professional negligence
- ✓ Loss of third party documents or data
- ✓ Unintentional breach of copyright and/or confidentiality
- ✓ Defamation and libel
- ✓ Loss of third party goods or money

Professional indemnity provides cover for the legal costs and expenses in defending such claims, as well as any compensation awarded to a third party.

In some countries, it is compulsory for all freelancers or the self-employed to carry professional indemnity insurance. Some dance schools provide professional indemnity for all their employees whether freelance or not, whereas others might insist the freelancers carry their own policies. This type of insurance cover can be a mandatory requirement for members of Dance Awarding Organisations and lead bodies. Some Dance Awarding Organisations offer access to policies as a member benefit.

Employer's liability

Employer's Liability insurance, also known as Workmen's Compensation in other countries, covers any liability that might be imposed on an employer if an employee is injured during the course of their employment. This insurance is compulsory in the United Kingdom if you employ someone with a contract of employment.

It may not be mandatory in other countries, but employee-led insurance claims can be expensive.

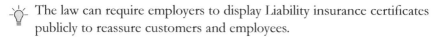 The law can require employers to display Liability insurance certificates publicly to reassure customers and employees.

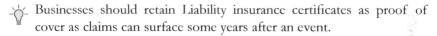 Businesses should retain Liability insurance certificates as proof of cover as claims can surface some years after an event.

Other policies

Other business policies to consider:

- **Employment Practices Liability** (EPL) insurance protects businesses against associated costs where, for example, an employee might take you, as the employer, to an employment tribunal for unfair dismissal
- **Business Interruption** following fire or disaster (against loss of profits)
- **Fidelity** including cash-in-transit, theft of equipment, dishonesty of employees
- **Key Person** insurance
- **Merchandise** insurance

The self-employed might wish to consider **Permanent Health Insurance** (PHI) as a safeguard against injury and ill health, which might affect their ability to run a business. This could be held in conjunction with **Key Person** insurance, referred to above. **Personal Accident and Sickness** (PA) insurance is an additional type of insurance that businesses can arrange for their employees as a benefit.

Now the business is up and running, Chapter 13 explores the operational aspects of your business.

OPERATING

Whether you are freelancer, as a teacher, artist, practitioner or a dance school owner you are a business and need to operate as a business to succeed. You will need to exercise business skills and take responsibility for aspects of the business such as:

- ✓ Marketing
- ✓ Development
- ✓ Finance
- ✓ Administration

While you might not be able to afford all the staff you need to cover some aspects of operations, someone has to be in charge. If you have staff, you will expect them to report to you and they will expect to be informed how they and the business are performing. Their targets will be set against your Business Plan.

This chapter looks at the skills and responsibilities you need to demonstrate.

Understanding the business

There are different types of business – service-led, such as a high-end super-market or a premium class of air travel; product-led, such as an iPhone or latest toy; or price-led, both at the top end and bottom end of the market. One of the characteristics of starting your own business is that you have to decide what type of business you want to be and the market you will be selling to.

Are you service-led, product-led or price-led.? What are you offering your customers? What is in it for them? Your customers will be buying the benefit of your business to them. This can help you to identify your Unique Selling Propositions (USPs) and influence your marketing strategy.

Bringing in the business

Marketing is the art of selling your business and your services to potential customers. Getting a message across. It needs to meet the needs of different sectors. You can do this by varying the services you offer, the prices you charge, the places you sell and the ways you promote.

How you get that message across depends on the approach you use. Placements can range from newspapers, magazines, radio and television, subscription services to websites, email, social media and apps. Methods can range from traditional print media – leaflets, brochures, handbooks, newsletters, advertising and promotions to digital media – blogs, webpages and texts.

Important aspects of offline, online and mobile planning are:

✓ SEO (Search Engine Optimisation): ensure that customers, both current and future, can find you

✓ Regular updates and posts: ensure that content is always fresh and up to date

✓ Brand consistency: ensure that your brand image is the same across all types of marketing

✓ Compliance: safeguarding, images, permissions and copyright

✓ Analytics: understand the traffic to your website

Marketing can provide the first, and often lasting, impression of your business. Without good marketing, your business may have no customers, or existing ones will fall away. The world is now very different from when businesses could rely on reputation alone or a lack of competition. The "high street" is rapidly changing.

Customers are mobile, street-wise and more demanding than ever. As discussed earlier, the best marketing tool can be you and your team.

Print

Leaflets, brochures, handbooks and newsletters do not have to be expensive, but the design and layout need to be simple and effective. Print media can be used for different purposes:

✓ Leaflets and flyers to publicise an event

✓ Brochures as a prospectus

✓ Handbooks to set out rules and regulations

✓ Newsletters to keep customers in touch

🔆 Ensure any externally produced print is also available as a pdf or word.doc so it can be used digitally on websites, social media and as attachments or links.

Merchandising can be used for marketing by displaying your logo and business name on t-shirts, uniforms and dance-related accessories.

Public relations

Promoting the school using the local media can cost you little or nothing if you can interest the local media in your business and its activities. Some of the steps to maximise this type of free publicity are:

✓ List all of the possible local media outlets: papers, radio, television

✓ Make the story: premiere choreography, exam results, dance performance, talented dancers and students, financial support, community and demographic involvement

✓ Identify your target: who is the audience?

✓ Issue a press release: who, what, where and when?

✓ Know your contact person at each of the media outlets

✓ Provide or arrange for a photo call

✓ Beat the print deadline

✓ Follow-up and get to know your contacts

✓ Keep in touch with your contacts

✓ Use the story on other media: website, social media, school newsletter

Advertising

Advertisements can be placed in local papers, magazines (dance, super-market, lifestyle, postcode specific), websites, social media, shop windows, notice boards (supermarkets, libraries, sports centres, coffee shops) etc. There are many opportunities to be noticed. Advertise wherever your target population is most likely to be looking and find a pattern of repeats that works.

Spend time discussing advertising copy and use of a brand/logo with the designers. It should reflect your target group. If you are promoting adult or older learner classes, use images of the mix you are looking for; likewise, if you are promoting dance classes for young people, use mixed gender photos to encourage young boys and girls. Promote diversity and equality.

 Ensure any brand/logo you commission is easy and cheap to reproduce so you can use it on print, merchandise and online media.

Look at other examples and figure out what is most eye-catching to you or others, or alternatively, why or what went wrong. If there are 100 advertisement cards in a shop window, consider how yours could stand out. Be aware of advertising standards, diversity and safeguarding issues. The key result from an advertisement should be the attention, interest, connection and contact from the customer.

 It can take time for a reader to notice your advertisement week to week. It should be eye-catching, bold, appropriate and clear.

It is more difficult to quantify the effectiveness of print advertising, whereas online advertisements can be linked to a click. You could set up a system to ask new contacts how they heard about your school and record and use the information to gauge what method has been the most effective.

Online advertising includes search-based advertising such as Google AdWords and Bing Ads, display advertising, as well as the online equivalents of local papers, print directories, magazines and notice boards.

Promotions

A way of keeping your business in the customer's eye can be to have promotions. For a dance school, promotions can range from "free taster classes", "bring a friend day", "refer a friend", "sibling discounts", "multiple class discounts", "3 for 2", " buy one get one free", "student of the month", "teacher of the month" to "choreographic competitions" and "prize draws". For a performance, promotions can range from "concessions for those in education and older patrons", "buy 10 seats for the price of 9" to "discounts for groups" and "matinee specials".

 Be careful about discounting too deeply. Discounts are essentially a lower price and do not necessarily increase revenue, especially if you have sufficient customers willing to pay full price.

Website

A website is an effective way to promote your business and as a teacher, artist and practitioner. Your target market needs to be able to find your website, and find it interesting and beneficial.

An effective website should provide information in an easy-to-navigate and easy-to-read manner. For a dance school if you need customers to register, consider having open content for first-time or nonregistered visitors which provides the information they are looking for, and enable them to register for a free taster class (if offered); and closed content for customers who attend your dance school and the classes you provide.

Open content could include information about the school, types of class, fees and timetables, application forms, etc. Closed content could be school events, payment methods, staff news, etc. Ensure that any content written directly onto the website can also be used for social media. Consider streaming photos from shows, video graduations and exam successes, set up a photo gallery.

Ensure that your website is compatible for mobile phones as well as laptops and PCs.

Email

Email is a very efficient and cost-effective substitute for print. All of the items identified as print material – leaflets, brochures, handbooks and newsletters – can be attached as a pdf attachment or linked to a website.

You can use email marketing software (EMS) such as MailChimp to create custom templates, newsletters, mailing lists and marketing campaigns. Email marketing is all about personalised messages that reach your customers at a time you want. The results can be measured and tested. Care needs to be taken about how you respond to enquiries resulting from marketing campaigns which can be overwhelming. Some EMS providers use auto-responders to assist in managing replies.

As your business grows, you can use online survey software such as SurveyMonkey to find out what your customers like, and what they might like more of.

 Be wary of too many surveys or questions that do not extract the right information. Many companies automatically survey hotels, flights, delivery which can lead to survey fatigue.

Social media

Social media or a social networking service is an internet platform on which a business can build a network for its customers to share information about the business, its activities, events, products and services, and human-interest stories. A powerful way to reach customers and meet marketing and branding goals is to create content for customers to view. Content can vary from blog or text to images and videos. With social media, you can:

✓ Raise brand awareness

✓ Encourage reviews and ratings

✓ Improve communication with current customers

✓ Obtain feedback from customers

✓ Compete effectively with competitors

✓ Increase interest in your services

✓ Grow the business

✓ Raise awareness of your website

There are many different social media platforms available, all with different characteristics. On the internet, you can find advice on which social media platform is best for which different types of message. Some of the most popular at the time of publication are: YouTube, Twitter, Instagram, LinkedIn, Snapchat, Baidu, Redditt, Google+, Pinterest, Facebook.

Having a commercial edge

Your business should have a commercial edge. You need to keep abreast of trends in the dance world, the latest teaching techniques and performance skills, as well as developments in technology that can help to drive the business.

Diversity can support your business. As *Chapter 2: Becoming Self-Employed* discussed, there are many options to offer within a dance school. This can vary from the number of genres, the levels offered, to the type of service and the age group.

Products and services

Neil Kokemuller (author of *Marketing as a Business System*) says, "diversification means branching out into other product categories, industries, or marketplaces. While this strategy does present some risks for a company, diversification is often viewed as a safety net against downturns in a single industry or a way to grow your business."[1] You should regularly ensure that you are offering the right type of classes, not only in genre but also in length, frequency, ability of staff, mix, time and popularity. This can be done

---

[1] (Kokemuller, 2018)

internally by monitoring your classes and customer surveys, and externally through your networks, magazines, life styles and trends.

External regulation

Chapters 9: Setting Fees and *12: Up and Running* discussed offering a regulated external examination stream within a school setting. This can be attractive to customers who want a recognised benchmark for their child's progress, as well as build up a learning portfolio of external dance qualifications.

Continuing professional development

Most teachers belong to a professional teaching body (Dance Awarding Organisation) that requires members to undertake annual mandatory continuing professional development. You can motivate your team by helping them to achieve this as part of your contract with them; and you can motivate your parents, carers and students with the achievements and quality of your team.

Continuing professional development also encompasses topics that will enhance the business and can include first aid, IT training, business techniques, safeguarding, data protection, customer service as well as teaching techniques and syllabus development.

Technology

There are apps available such as Eventbrite, a US-based event management and ticketing website, which can be used to offer potential customers a place on a taster class, or fill unfilled places in walk-in classes, one-off workshops, or events.

Controlling your money

Balancing the flow of money through your business is a key to success. How you collect money is vital, as customers are often busy and may not always be punctual with paying bills. This affects cash flow. Emailing invoices and state-ments in portable document format (PDF) to your customers is generally more time- and cost-effective.

The use of early bird discounts, payment packages and late payment surcharges can assist in timely payment as well as using online payments and payment service providers (PSPs) to speed up payment.

Some businesses outsource the payment of invoices to a factor company. This is known as invoice factoring. It is a form of business financing whereby a business sells their Accounts Receivable (invoices) to a factor company who collect payment from the Debtor (customer). The factor company in turn provides the business with an upfront fixed amount of the total invoice value within a specified time, and the balance (less charges) at a later date.

Bank accounts and credit cards

It is advisable to have a separate business bank account so you can easily distinguish business and personal income and expenditure. Credit card agreements do not normally allow personal credit cards to be used for business purposes.

Record keeping

By law, you usually have to maintain and retain accounting records for up to six or seven years. Electronic bookkeeping is quick and convenient and provides additional features that can help you understand your finances and run your business more effectively. Receipts and invoices should be retained as proof of purchase and sale.

Accounting and bookkeeping procedures need to be sound, accurate and timely, with controls over who enters the data, who is responsible for paying suppliers, employees and freelancers, who collects your debts, and who produces financial reports.

Record keeping may have to meet minimum standards, especially if you are registered for value added or sales tax.

 If you have concerns about your skills in this area, engage a bookkeeper or accountant to take care of budgets, accounting records and bookkeeping.

You need to choose an accounting year-end. In the United Kingdom, the tax year (fiscal year) ends on 5th April. It is generally easier for an accounting year to end at the same time as the fiscal year. However, for dance schools this would mean that an accounting year would end at the end of the spring term and start at the beginning of the summer term. Having a 5th April year-end can complicate the analysis of fees, costs and student numbers for budgets and forecasts if fee increases, staff recruitment and staff salary increases coincided with an academic year starting in September.

 As a dance school, it would make sense to have an accounting year-end that coincides with the end of the summer term. Your annual Accounts would then be for a full school year. You should check with your professional adviser the best way to accomplish this.

In the United Kingdom, it is possible to choose a date that suits you. Other countries have different fiscal and academic years while some countries may require all businesses to have the same year-end.

Budgets and cash flow

You should use budgets to control your money and your business. Ensure you receive regular monthly updates of actual against budget. If you are responsible for this, you must be strict and get into the habit of comparing performance against budget and identifying what is going wrong and how it can be improved. As discussed in *Chapter 6: Using Financial Tools*, budgets can be revised during a financial year.

Get in the habit of preparing budgets each year. Ideally, you should be one budget ahead all of the time.

Control your cash flow. Chase up late payers and do not rush to pay suppliers. Use your break-even analysis to ensure you are generating sufficient cash.

Pricing

Ensure that your pricing policy is clear and includes information about discounts and refunds. Ensure that prices are regularly reviewed.

Merchandise

If you are selling merchandise, ensure that there is control over stock, who orders, when they order, and how much they order. You should use technology to reduce your costs so that you can compete on price and delivery. Over-supply can lead to slow-moving stock and loss of return on money invested.

Consider creating your own uniform colour, selling examination wear and associated dancewear. For example, International Dance Supplies, an online dancewear company, sells to dance teachers at prices encouraging them to operate their own shops. Freed of London, based in London and New York, sells a wide range of dance and ballet wear through stockists and offers teachers of the Royal Academy of Dance, a DAO based in London, a discount through their online shop. Other Dance Awarding Organisations have agreements with manufacturers who offer dance supplies at discounted prices.

Alternatively, you could set up your own arrangements with a local dancewear shop and earn commission on referrals.

Consider the advantages of an online shop against a more traditional shopfront. You could use stock to promote your wares, with online purchases only.

Technology

Accounting software packages should be flexible enough to communicate with your customers online, and enable them to access their account information. In turn, customers can respond or pay you in the most flexible and efficient manner. Use technology to turn slow payers to your advantage. Consider mobile payment companies such as iZettle or Square, and payment service providers (PSP) such as PayPal, ApplePay and others, in order to accept mobile electronic payments from your customers.

PSPs generally cover a variety of payment methods including credit card, direct debits, bank transfers and real-time bank transfers based on online banking, which suit most customers.

Take advantage of apps such as Coconut, Squirrel and Chip which are using "open banking" rules that allow them, with your consent, to analyse your expenditure data to, *e.g.,* suggest ways of saving money; manage your business income and expenses, VAT and tax; or create budgets based on historic spend.

 Ensure that whatever apps you choose and consent to are regulated by the Financial Conduct Authority (FCA) or equivalent and are secure.

 Many other apps can send receipts for online transactions.

Controlling your business

Administration controls the business. It is the art of pulling all these factors together – building on marketing campaigns, implementing development ideas, linking technology, motivating teaching staff and customers, getting the money in, as well as the day-to-day concerns of ensuring your dance school runs to schedule, with working equipment, clean studios and a full complement of staff.

Each part of the business has its own importance, and as a small business owner, you will most likely be responsible for these. This can be a tremendous challenge and can become even more daunting with the day-to-day running of the business.

Customer service

The key to drawing all this together is good customer service. Customers can be demanding, but they have the right to be. You are selling a service, and they are buying it. You will lose potential customers if the service is below standard or not what they want.

For dance schools, customers are students, parents, or carers. These customers will have different needs. A student will want to be taught well, feel they are in safe hands, value for money and, above all, enjoy themselves. A parent or carer, on the other hand, might want access to nearby parking, good transport, friendly staff, value for money and somewhere to get a coffee. In a dance school, your customers could be with you for the long term. If a student starts with Pre-school classes and is a promising dancer you could realistically expect the student to be still with you aged 16 or 17, providing there had been no change in the student's circumstances. This is a longer life cycle than most products.

You must provide what was promised, dependably, accurately and consistently; you must be able to respond to customers promptly; you must be seen as trustworthy, competent, value for money and confident; must show your customers you care; and your business, staff, studio and equipment should reflect this. It is essential that all staff, whether front of house or teaching staff, look after your resources well – including themselves – and deliver good customer service by promoting reliability, responsiveness, assurance and empathy.

Customer care can take many forms, from customer surveys, student feedback, internal and external assessment, parent and carer observation days, to you and your staff displaying a positive, listening and caring persona.

It is good practice to have a written complaints procedure. This procedure can be included in your prospectus and on a website so that both staff and customers are aware of what to do in case of a complaint. Written procedures help you to tackle complaints in a consistent and controlled way.

Policies and procedures

In today's environment, businesses need to have sound policies and procedures in place. Good practice can dictate that a business has the following policies, which can apply equally to employees, freelancers, volunteers, customers and visitors:

✓ Health and Safety
✓ Data Protection
✓ Safeguarding young people and vulnerable adults
✓ Equality and Diversity

These policies tend to be linked. For example, Data Protection and Equality and Diversity policies support not only a Safeguarding young people and vulnerable adults policy, but also clauses within employee, freelance and volunteer contracts relating to dignity and respect at work, and disciplinary matters.

Chapter 14: Complying with the Law explores these policies in more detail.

As businesses grow, legislation may provide mandatory requirements on publishing and implementing certain policies and procedures.

The law often requires employers to display certain types of certificates such as employer insurance, liability insurance, data protection and emergency procedures.

Many schools publish a Prospectus, which can set out information about the business, its ethos, its products and services, the academic year, prices and payment, uniform policy, and associated rules and regulations of attendance. A prospectus can be both printed and digital, and can be known as a Handbook.

 Parents, carers and students are often required to sign a form, which acts as both an enrolment form and an acceptance of the dance school rules and regulations of attendance. If customers can enrol online, the digital copy should state that submission means that the rules and regulations have been accepted, and considered signed as if physically.

The possible contents of a school prospectus are contained in *Chapter 15: Attracting Customers*.

Staffing

Team meetings should be a vehicle through which the health of the business is discussed and resolved. It is good practice to hold them regularly. You may wish to have joint as well as separate meetings between administrative and teaching staff. The beginning of term can be a good time, followed by a mid-term meeting to determine progress and discuss issues and concerns.

All staff should know the policies and procedures, rules and regulations, of your dance school and put them into practice. Ensure that you know how your staff are feeling, ask them to contribute to the agenda for meetings. This enables you to exercise control while at the same time hearing any of their concerns.

Ensure that overall staffing needs are regularly reviewed. This should include those already employed by you and those who you may wish to hire in the future. Periodically review the criteria for hiring staff, and review legal contracts to ensure compliance and best practice.

Every business has its own topics to discuss, but consider having standard subject headings at every meeting, when topics can be discussed, for example:

Staffing

- ✓ Administrative staff
- ✓ Teaching staff
- ✓ Volunteers
- ✓ Changes in staff
- ✓ Continuing professional development
- ✓ Appraisals

Studios

- ✓ Resources and equipment
- ✓ Maintenance and cleanliness
- ✓ Security
- ✓ First aid

Students

- ✓ Registers and timeliness of students
- ✓ Current enrolment and retention
- ✓ Free tasters and conversion rate
- ✓ Leavers and understanding why

Marketing

- ✓ Success of current promotions
- ✓ Upcoming promotions
- ✓ Advertising campaigns
- ✓ Content of website and suggestions for improvement
- ✓ Current handbook and suggestions for improvement

Finance

- ✓ Meeting forecasts and budgets
- ✓ Fees collection, overdue accounts
- ✓ Policy on barring students
- ✓ Expenses and overruns

Administration

- ✓ Mix of classes, lesson plans
- ✓ Rules and regulations, changes and application
- ✓ Policies and procedures, changes and implementation
- ✓ Difficult parents and complaints
- ✓ Insurance

Merchandise

- ✓ Sale of merchandise
- ✓ School uniform

Any other matters

Consider using technology for your internal communication, using apps such as Telegram for instant messaging; Slack for meetings and sharing files with staff; Zoom, for video conferencing, on-line meetings, chat, and mobile collaboration; and Lucid for goal setting, improving mental awareness and focus.

Unique Selling Propositions (USPs)

Try to identify anything that will make your business stand out from your competitors – even in a crowded market place with similar products and services. It is the proposition that is important and not necessarily having a unique product or service.

Entrepreneur.com defines a Unique Selling Proposition: as "The factor or consideration presented by a seller as the reason that one product or service is different from and better than that of the competition."[2]

When starting out, you will not have many customers to ask, but from your research, you should be able to identify some of the characteristics that drive customers to dance schools. Be careful to offer a stable range of dance genres to underpin the business.

You can discover your USP by:

- Putting yourself in your customers' shoes.

    Why will your customers come to your dance school? What will make them sign up for classes? What will make them return each term? What will give satisfaction to your customers? The answer might be

---

[2] (Entrepreneur Magazine, 2018)

good teaching, "star" guest teachers, previous external exam success, approachability, safety, reliability, friendliness, or customer service, good feedback, convenience, location, friendships.

● Understanding your customers' behaviour and buying decisions.

Why will your customers buy your classes? What will drive and motivate them? It could be peer pressure, making friends, acquiring life skills, fashion, fitness, or the latest trend.

● Uncovering the real reasons customers favour your classes.

As your business grows, ask customers why they prefer your school to others.

When you have gone through these steps, the task is to identify and promote those features that might set you apart and make customers want to patronise your business. Base your USPs on the four elements that make up your marketing mix:

✓ The products and services you offer

✓ The prices you charge

✓ The places you sell

✓ The ways you deliver

Some ideas to explore:

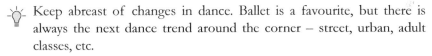 Keep abreast of changes in dance. Ballet is a favourite, but there is always the next dance trend around the corner – street, urban, adult classes, etc.

 Price is not always the only reason customers might come to class.

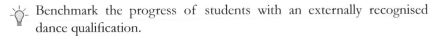 Consider a free leotard service for children – aimed at those parents who are unable to afford to buy new leotards to satisfy Dance Awarding Organisation uniform requirements. Parent to parent "second-hand cupboard" works well.

🔆 Benchmark the progress of students with an externally recognised dance qualification.

🔆 Help disadvantaged students.

🔆 Help gifted and talented students.

🔆 Employ qualified and motivated staff.

🔆 Promote a life-long learning environment to staff, students and customers.

- ☀ Support good causes and local charities through school events.

- ☀ Engage with local community and services.

- ☀ Attract different audiences with different social media platforms.

- ☀ Promote the safety and well-being of students.

If you get this right, then you are essentially selling you and your business, which is at the heart of your USPs.

COMPLYING WITH THE LAW

KEY POINTS

Code of Conduct and Professional Practice   Health and Safety   Data Protection
Safeguarding young people and vulnerable adults   Equality and Diversity   Compliance

This chapter looks at codes, policies and procedures that dance businesses need to be aware of. In some countries, it is not mandatory to have certain statements and policies. It can be good practice to adopt them, *e.g.*, "the EU's 2018 General Data Protection Regulation (GDPR) is effectively becoming a global benchmark for privacy regulation".[1]

Most teaching organisations[2] and dance professional bodies have Codes of Conduct and Professional Practice that their members and registered teachers abide by as a condition of their membership and registration. The complexity of legislation and legal frameworks, litigation, and increased scrutiny by governments emphasises the importance of ethical practice and commitment. These Codes often refer to the type of environment in which dance schools should operate, the standards they should set, and the statements and policies they should follow. It is essential that dance schools adhere to a Code of Conduct and Professional Practice on which customers can rely.

Young people and vulnerable adults can form a large part of a dance business customer base. Increasingly legislation imposes regulations on businesses that work in this field, concerning issues such as:

● Health and Safety

● Data Protection

● Safeguarding young people and vulnerable adults

● Equality and Diversity

---

[1]   (Benady, 2018)
[2]   Appendix 4

A Statement should set out what the business believes in, and a Policy states how the statement is put into practice. This chapter examines potential Statements and Policies relating to these issues. These should be viewed as "specimen only", and dance owners should seek appropriate advice to determine the content and completeness of such Statements and Policies.

Health and Safety

There will be legislation that sets out whether or not you are required to have a written statement and policy. In the UK, current legislation states that all businesses employing five or more people must have a written health and safety policy statement.[3] The policy should cover all aspects of the business and be relevant to your employees and customers. The definition of employees should be extended to freelancers and volunteers contracted by the dance school.

A Health and Safety Policy will demonstrate how seriously your business takes health and safety responsibilities. A good policy will show how your business protects those who could be affected by your activities.

The policy should be of an appropriate length and relevance to the activities and size of your business. Typically, it would include two or three elements:

○ A Statement section that demonstrates your business's commitment to health and safety; and

○ A Policy section that contains details of how specific activities and functions are managed and put into operation. This section could include such matters as risk assessments, fire safety, first aid and accident reporting. Other matters might be included if relevant, such as electrical safety, work equipment, hazardous substances, manual handling and other workplace issues.

○ The Policy section could also include a sub-section or a third section on the allocation of responsibilities and how employees, freelancers and volunteers fit into the overall safety management system.

For a dance school, a risk assessment of the dance space is crucial. Employees or freelancers who are responsible for the classes should ensure that the space is safe and fit for purpose as part of their duties.

---

[3] At time of publication

Specimen statement

For example, a Health and Safety Statement might read:

> "*XYZDanz* is committed to learning from all accidents and incidents in order to continuously improve the delivery of health and safety within the school. We are also committed to protecting our employees, freelancers, volunteers and customers as far as is reasonably practicable, and complying with (*insert name of relevant health and safety legislation*) and all associated safety legislation and regulations and industry good practice.
>
> We aim to achieve the highest standards of health, safety and welfare for all classes and activities within our control so that staff, visitors, customers, parents, carers, suppliers, and others who may be affected by classes and activities and operations within the school are, so far as is reasonably possible, not exposed to hazards and thereby protected from risks.
>
> Our full policy can be found on *XYZDanz*'s website (give reference)."

Policy

A Health and Safety Policy should follow relevant legislation and regulations. Such policies, with or without legislation, should refer inter alia to:

- ✓ Accident books
- ✓ Recording incidents
- ✓ Responding to incidents
- ✓ First aid stations
- ✓ Staff training
- ✓ Emergency procedures
- ✓ Attendance registers
- ✓ Risk assessments
- ✓ Applicability
- ✓ Who does what
- ✓ Complaint procedures
- ✓ Review date

Advice regarding the preparation of statements and policies and in conducting risk assessments can be found on the internet, as well as the UK Government's Health and Safety Executive (HSE).[4]

---

[4] (Health and Safety Executive, 2018)

Data Protection[5]

The UK's Data Protection Act is based on the General Data Protection Regulation (Regulation (EU) 2016/679) which apply to all businesses regardless of size that collect or process personal data and enshrine an individual's right:

✓ To be informed

✓ Of access

✓ To rectification

✓ To erasure

✓ To restrict processing

✓ To data portability

✓ To object

✓ Not to be subject to automated decision making including profiling

Businesses, located outside the EU, may wish to consider following EU data rules as the practical and commercial risks of not having a policy can limit access to markets and damage a "brand". There are eight basic principles of collection and processing which state that personal data must be:

✓ Obtained fairly and lawfully

✓ Obtained for one or more specified and lawful purpose

✓ Adequate, relevant, and not excessive for those purposes

✓ Accurate and kept up to date

✓ Kept for no longer than is necessary for those purposes

✓ Processed in line with the rights of the data subject

✓ Secured against accidental loss, destruction, damage, unauthorised or unlawful processing

✓ Transferred only to countries inside the European Economic Area, unless the country outside has equivalent levels of protection

A dance business that collects the personal data of students, parents, carers, employees, guest teachers, freelancers and volunteers would be considered a data controller under the regulations and would need to disclose:

✓ Why the data is collected?

✓ How personal data is used?

[5] (Information Commissioner's Office (ICO), 2018)

✓ How long it is held?

✓ That it is held securely

✓ What happens in the event of a data breach?

✓ What happens when a right to access data is exercised?

The regulations lay down six lawful bases for processing:

✓ Clear consent has been given for a specific purpose

✓ Contract or pre-contract terms exist between the business and the individual

✓ Legal (other than contractual) obligation

✓ Protection of life

✓ Public interest (and a clear basis in law)

✓ Legitimate interest

Consent has to be active rather than passive, opt-in rather than opt-out. Data Protection Statement and Policies, more often referred to as Privacy Statements and Policies, should clearly set out all of the above.

Specimen statement

A Privacy Statement should summarise why you need to collect the data, how you will use it, how long you intend to keep it, how you will look after it, and how the individual can access their data.

For example, a Privacy Statement might read:

"Any personal information you provide will be processed in accordance with (*insert name of relevant data protection legislation*). *XYZDanz* will use the information to create an electronic and paper record of your application; to enable the application to be processed; to provide information about our current and future activities; to assist in our marketing and to enable us to compile statistics or to assist other organisations where legally required to do so, provided that no statistical information would identify you as an individual. The information will be kept securely, and will be kept no longer than necessary.

Our full Privacy Policy including our contact details and your rights to access can be found on *XYZDanz*'s website (give reference)."

Statements should be included on any form (paper or digital) where you collect data. You might wish to have slightly different statements for the following:

✓ Employee application forms

✓ Freelance contract details

✓ Volunteer application forms

✓ Student enrolment forms

✓ Event attendance forms

✓ Customer payment forms

✓ Supplier contract details

The importance of Statements is that they inform employees, freelancers, volunteers, students, payees and suppliers how you will use their data.

Policy

A Privacy Policy is a more detailed explanation of the Statement and discloses the lawful basis (or bases, if more than one applies) for processing and the intended purposes for processing. A policy needs to follow any legislative and regulatory requirements,

A policy should provide clear information, guidance and reasoning on the following points:

✓ What information do we collect about you, and how?

✓ How will we use the information about you, and why?

✓ Why and what we contact you for and about (marketing)?

✓ How you can access information we hold about you?

✓ Your right to correction and opting out

✓ What are cookies and how we use them

✓ What our relationship and your data is to other websites

✓ When we review and change our Privacy Policy

✓ How we safeguard your data

✓ Who is the Data Controller?

✓ Who are the Data Processors?

✓ Staff training in handling data

✓ Our contact details

Safeguarding young people and vulnerable adults

Your school will attract young people to the classes, and classes for adults and older learners could attract vulnerable adults. The term *safeguarding* is broader than 'child protection' and relates to the action taken to promote the welfare of children and vulnerable adults to protect them from harm.

Safeguarding is everyone's responsibility at a school and includes:

- ✓ Protecting children and vulnerable adults from maltreatment
- ✓ Preventing impairment of the health and development of children and vulnerable adults
- ✓ Ensuring that children grow up in circumstances consistent with the provision of safe and effective care
- ✓ Enabling all children and vulnerable adults to have the best possible outcomes

Safeguarding would include a child protection policy and procedures for dealing with issues of concern or abuse.

Specimen statement

For example, a Safeguarding Statement might read:

"*XYZDanz* is committed to promoting the health, development, safety and welfare of all young people and vulnerable adults attending classes and activities. We recognise that we serve a diverse community at our school including culture, race, ethnicity, religion, social class, financial resources, and ability.

Our commitment is to work in partnership with parents and carers regarding safeguarding concerns of any young people and vulnerable adults.

We are committed to protecting all young people and vulnerable adults as far as is reasonably practical in accordance with (*insert name of any relevant legislation or guidelines*).

Our full policy can be found on *XYZDanz*'s website (give reference)."[6]

Policy

A Safeguarding Policy needs to follow the pertinent legislative and regulatory requirements. Advice can be found on the internet. Documents can be complex and safeguarding procedures can differ by county, province or state and professional advice should be sought. The following key questions need to be considered when writing a policy:

---

[6] Reference could also be given to the Equality and Diversity policy

✓ What are the potential risks to children – who may pose a risk?

✓ What situations may increase risk?

✓ How do you check people who work at the school?

✓ How do you check people who come into contact with students?

✓ How do you ensure that your students leave the premises safely?

✓ What are the different ways someone might raise a concern?

✓ How should you respond to concerns or allegations of harm?

✓ How does your policy link up with other policies and procedures?

✓ How do you train your employees, freelancers and volunteers?

✓ How will you raise awareness for everyone involved with the organisation?

Such policies, with or without legislation, should make inter alia references to:

✓ Applicability

✓ Confidentiality

✓ Physical contact in class

✓ Recognition and signs of abuse

✓ Recording incidents

✓ Responding to incidents

✓ Staff training, recruitment, selection and vetting

✓ Health and Safety

✓ Emergency procedures

✓ Use of, and consent to, photography, and use of images and videos

✓ Protection online

✓ Equality and Diversity

✓ Anti-bullying

✓ Review date

Equality and Diversity

In an increasingly diverse society, equality and diversity influences all aspects of our lives and work. You need to be able to respond appropriately and sensitively to this diversity.

● Equality is about creating a fairer society, where everyone can participate and has the opportunity to fulfil their potential. An equalities approach understands that who we are – based on gender, race, disability, age, social class, sexuality, or religion – can affect our life experiences.

For example, class segregation. Young girls traditionally make up almost 100% of dance classes, but more boys are taking up dance. Your classes and dance school should be attractive to young boys to encourage participation and to remove stereotypes. Your older learner classes recognise that the older person can participate in such an activity.

● Diversity literally means difference. When it is used as a contrast or in addition to equality, it is about considering, recognising and understanding individual, as well as group, differences. People should be treated as individuals with positive emphasis placed on diversity both in the community and in the workforce. Employers through flexible working patterns, adaptive workstations, are increasingly recognising background, personality, work style etc.

In many countries, there is a diversity of backgrounds, and dance schools may wish to explain to those involved in dance, for example, why a dance uniform may differ because of different cultural, religious or ethnic considerations.

Specimen statement

For example, an Equality and Diversity Statement might state:

"At *XYZDanz* the diversity of our employees, classes and activities is at the heart of our values and objectives. We are committed to equality of opportunity and freedom from discrimination in our employment and the classes and activities we provide.

Our policy aims to ensure that all employees, freelancers, volunteers, students and customers are treated fairly and encouraged to reach their full potential regardless of gender, marital status, parental status, disability, age, race, colour, nationality, ethnicity, religion, sexual orientation, or political affiliation.

Our full policy can be found on *XYZDanz*'s website (give reference)."

Policy

An Equality and Diversity Policy needs to follow any legislative and regulatory requirements. Advice can found on the internet, but documents can be complex so professional advice should be sought.

Discrimination can take seven main forms: direct discrimination; associative discrimination; discrimination by perception; indirect discrimination including harassment, victimisation and bullying through prejudice; ignorance; thoughtlessness; stereotyping.

There are also nine protected characteristics: age, disability, gender reassignment, race (including colour, nationality and ethnicity), religion or belief, sex, sexual orientation, marriage and civil partnership, pregnancy and maternity.

Such policies, with or without legislation, should refer to not only the types of discrimination and the protected characteristics but also inter alia to:

- ✓ Impartiality of employment-related policies, practices and procedures
- ✓ Impartiality of customer-related policies, practices and procedures
- ✓ Equality of staff opportunity
- ✓ Breaches of attitudes and behaviour
- ✓ Work/life balance measures
- ✓ Complaints and incident handling
- ✓ Staff training
- ✓ Accountability and responsibility
- ✓ Review date

All school policies should be designed to promote equal opportunity and protection against discrimination for all employees, freelancers, volunteers and customers, as far as practical.

Compliance

Examples of good and bad Statements and Policies can be found online.

Laws and regulations are complex, and while advice can be found on the internet, business owners should recognise that over time statements and policies may become modified, amended or changed by the requirements of the law, and statements and policies of equal importance may be added.

Your Dance Awarding Organisation may assist in these, but you are strongly advised to subscribe to networks that will keep you informed of statutory changes, undertake regular reviews, and take professional advice when drawing up and amending Statements and Policies.

Statements and Policies should be easily accessed by your employees, freelancers, volunteers, customers and visitors *e.g.,* displayed on notice boards, published on your website and shared with customers when they supply personal details in person or on the telephone.

CHAPTER 15

ATTRACTING CUSTOMERS

KEY POINTS

Welcome statement   Aims and ethos   Products and services   Enrolment procedures
Attendance   Classes   Safeguarding   Facilities   Fees   Code of Customer Behaviour
Legal   Contact

This chapter sets out the possible content that could be included in a School Prospectus. (A Business Prospectus is usually referred to in the context of the stock market and providing information to prospective investors.)

A School Prospectus is a document available for prospective students and customers telling them about the business. It can be an excellent way to communicate with your customers. It ideally sets out information about the school, its ethos, products and services, the academic year, prices and payment, uniform, and associated rules and regulations regarding attendance.

A Prospectus can be printed and digital, glossy or plain, and may be known as a Handbook. It can be accompanied by an application or enrolment form, which, when signed by the parent, carer, attendee or payee, signifies acceptance of the terms and conditions under which the school operates.

 If customers can enrol online, the digital copy should state that an electronic submission indicates that the rules and regulations have been read, understood and accepted, and that electronic submission carries the same importance as if the application or enrolment had been physically signed.

The headings, set out below, are intended only as an aide-memoire. They may or may not be applicable for all dance schools, additional information may be necessary and some schools may decide to provide the information in other formats, different layouts, headings, or order.

- Welcome statement
- Aims and ethos statement, including
  - ✓ USPs (Unique Selling Propositions)
  - ✓ Gifted and talented students

- Product and services, covering
  - ✓ Genres offered
  - ✓ Classes offered
  - ✓ Other activities
  - ✓ External accreditation and competitions
  - ✓ Employees and their qualifications
  - ✓ Use of volunteers
  - ✓ Code of Conduct and Professional Practice
- Enrolment procedures, covering
  - ✓ How to apply
  - ✓ Taster classes and assessments
  - ✓ Initial and continuing enrolment
  - ✓ Starting dates
  - ✓ Withdrawal and cancellation policy
  - ✓ Minimum/maximum class numbers
  - ✓ Waiting lists
  - ✓ Parents and carers
  - ✓ Health disclosure
  - ✓ Equality and Diversity statement
  - ✓ Accuracy of information
- Attendance, covering
  - ✓ Arrival and departure, start and finish
  - ✓ Class registration
  - ✓ Attendance
  - ✓ Discipline
  - ✓ Punctuality
  - ✓ Uniform and dress etiquette
  - ✓ Medical absence
  - ✓ Additional classes
  - ✓ External assessments
  - ✓ Mainstream school absence letter
- Classes, covering
  - ✓ Class timetable

- ✓ Examination timetable
- ✓ Teacher/s
- ✓ Classroom assistants
- ✓ Class observation
- ✓ Cancellation and changes
- ✓ Toilets/facilities
- ✓ Code of conduct in class
- ✓ Drinking liquids in studio
- Safeguarding, covering
  - ✓ Safeguarding statement
  - ✓ Privacy and use of CCTV (closed circuit television)
  - ✓ Use of mobiles, cells and photography
  - ✓ Photographic and video consent
  - ✓ Policy on physical contact in class
  - ✓ Supervision in class
- Facilities, covering
  - ✓ Location of the school
  - ✓ How to find us
  - ✓ Reception and registration
  - ✓ Studios
  - ✓ Changing rooms
  - ✓ Waiting area
  - ✓ Food and drink on premises
  - ✓ Personal property
  - ✓ Accident book
  - ✓ Cleaning book
  - ✓ Parking
  - ✓ Emergency procedures
  - ✓ Health and Safety statement
- Fees, covering
  - ✓ Definition of payee
  - ✓ Fee schedule
  - ✓ Discounts

- ✓ Refunds
- ✓ Methods of payment
- ✓ How to pay
- ✓ When to pay
- ✓ Outstanding fees
- ✓ Debt collection
- ✓ Late payment and non-payment
- ✓ Cost of additional classes
- ✓ Cost of external assessment
- ✓ Financial assistance
- Code of Customer Behaviour, covering
  - ✓ Respect and understanding
  - ✓ Safety
  - ✓ Confidentiality
  - ✓ Inappropriate social media posting
  - ✓ Physical and verbal threats and attacks
  - ✓ Abusive and offensive behaviour
  - ✓ Smoking and alcohol on premises
  - ✓ Interference
  - ✓ Breaches, redress and appeals
- Legal, covering
  - ✓ Status of school
  - ✓ Business name
  - ✓ Registration numbers
  - ✓ Copyright
  - ✓ Trade marks
  - ✓ Liability for damage
  - ✓ Right to reserve
  - ✓ Waivers
  - ✓ Complaints procedure
  - ✓ Privacy statement (Data Protection)
  - ✓ Written and online agreement
  - ✓ Changes in consumption tax rates

- ✓ Legal jurisdiction
- Contact, covering
  - ✓ How to contact
  - ✓ Who to contact
  - ✓ Responsible officers
  - ✓ Website
  - ✓ Social media

ENGAGING FREELANCERS

This chapter sets out typical clauses in an agreement made between a business and a freelancer. The content and substance of the clauses are provided to give general guidance regarding the terms on which a dance school might engage a self-employed teacher or conversely what a freelancer might expect in a Contract *for* Services.

The clauses are generally suitable for businesses that contract teachers who are self-employed, and provide a basis on which a suitable agreement can be based and legal advice sought.

Guidance

Agreements should be carefully drawn up. Of particular importance is the clarity of cancellation clauses for both parties. If classes have to be cancelled, dance schools should ensure that they provide, or a self-employed teacher receives, sufficient notice so that the self-employed teacher can obtain other work before a new term starts, otherwise compensation might be required.

 Adequate notification could be linked to a time period before the start of a term.

Dance schools might wish to consider whether to include a restrictive covenant in an agreement. Such clauses restrict a teacher, after leaving a dance school, from attempting to take staff or students with them. Terms may also state that the teacher cannot carry on competition within a specified radius of the school. Such covenants would be binding only if they protect the legitimate business interests of the dance school towards its students and staff.

If the restrictive covenant went further than is strictly necessary, for example, because the period is too long or because the catchment area is too wide, then the covenant would not be enforceable, although it might still act as a deterrent.

As discussed in *Chapters 5: Choosing a Business Structure* and *11: Paying Taxes*, the self-employed are liable for their own tax and social insurance payments. However, the nature of the agreement with the dance school may influence an individual's tax status. As previously stated, the tax authorities may look beyond the words of the agreement to decide whether a teacher is properly self-employed.

 A self-employed teacher should generally have more than one source of income to be considered as self-employed by the tax authorities although this may differ from country to country, or change with the law.

The tax authorities could decide that a freelancer is actually an employee and that the dance school should have been deducting tax and social insurance, which could result in a substantial amount being due by the dance school to the tax authorities.

 An indemnity clause in an agreement to cover such claims is only as good as the ability to seek payment from the teacher.

Dance schools should try to satisfy themselves beforehand that a teacher is properly regarded as self-employed.

 This might be evidenced by a taxpayer identification number (TIN/ UTR) or confirmation by the freelancer's accountant.

Terms of engagement

The following headings and sub-headings are not intended to be exhaustive and represent what might be typically included. Some of these terms may be similar to what you expect of an employee.

- Personal details
  - Name
  - Address
  - Contact number
- Contract type
  - Engagement as (*freelance teacher*)
  - Contract start and end date

○ Status and relationship

State that the status will be self-employed and that the relationship will be as an independent contractor, indicating that there is no employee relationship.

○ Absence

Describe how sickness absences should be reported, indicating how, when, and to whom.

Describe how requests for planned absences should be made, indicating how, when, and to whom.

● Remuneration

○ Fees payable (*per hour, per class, per week, per term*)

Break down the fees into different categories if there are payments for class, attending staff meetings, examination or external assessment days, working additional hours, writing reports, etc.

○ Expenses reimbursement

State which expenses might be reimbursed, indicating what conditions might be attached to reimbursement.

○ Travelling expenses

State what travel might be reimbursed, indicating what conditions might be attached to claiming (class of public transport, use of own car).

○ Deductions

State what deductions might be deducted from any amounts due.

🔆 You might request the right of set-off if the freelancer owes the business for a service.

🔆 Some jurisdictions might consider a freelancer eligible for mandatory pension provision.

● Activity

○ Class

Describe the classes you wish the contractor to teach (and demonstrate), indicating the term, dates, times including breaks, and location(s).

○ Reports

State whether you will require reports, questionnaires or other types of information on the classes or students taught, or both.

○ Registers

State whether you will require the class register maintained, indicating when, how, and why; and if not, then state who is responsible for the registers.

○ Supervision pre- and post-class

State whether you will require students to be collected and returned before and after class. Indicate when, how, where from/back to and, if not, state who is responsible for supervision.

○ Supervision in class

State whether you will supply an assistant in the class for additional supervision, indicating which classes.

○ Staff meetings

State whether you will require attendance at staff meetings, indicating frequency, timing and contribution.

○ Taster days, open days and observation days

Describe how taster, open and observation days might work.

○ Other services

Describe whether there are any circumstances where activities might be added to the engagement and what terms might apply.

● Policies

○ Code of Conduct and Professional Practice

State that the engagement is subject to compliance with the (*insert name of relevant organisation*) Code of Conduct and Professional Practice, indicating location of the Code of Conduct and Professional Practice.

 If the freelancer belongs to an organisation that has its own Code of Conduct and Professional Practice, then you could state that the higher standard would prevail.

○ Rules and Regulations of the School

State that the engagement is subject to compliance with the school's internal Rules and Regulations, indicating location of the Rules and Regulations.

○ Data Privacy

State that the engagement is subject to confidentiality and compliance with the school's Privacy policy, indicating location of the Policy and any restrictions during and after the contract ends.

Describe responsibilities, which might include disclosing or making use of any secret or confidential information belonging to the school; or personal or sensitive information relating to students, staff or volunteers other than the purposes for which it was originally intended.

○ Health and Safety

State that the engagement is subject to compliance with the school's Health and Safety policy, indicating location of the Policy.

Describe responsibilities, which might include risk assessments, familiarisation with emergency procedures, a safe environment, prevention and reporting of accidents, and reasonable care.

○ Safeguarding young people and vulnerable adults

State that the engagement is subject to compliance with the school's Safeguarding policy, indicating location of the Policy. Describe responsibilities, which can include obtaining clearance (DBS[1] or equivalent) to work with children, training in safeguarding, co-operating and assisting with investigations, etc.

○ Equality and Diversity

State that the engagement is subject to compliance with the school's Equality and Diversity policy, indicating location of Policy.

Describe responsibilities, which might include treating all students, customers, employees, freelancers and volunteers with the same dignity and respect.

● Cancellation, supply and termination

○ Cancellation

Describe when the school might cancel an engagement either absolutely or with a substitution, indicating reason, sufficient notification, substitution basis and payment terms.

○ Supply teaching

State that the performance of this engagement may or may not be sub-contracted, transferred or assigned, indicating when or how a replacement teacher might be brought in or alternative arrangements made if they fell ill, and the payment terms.

○ Termination

Describe how the contract can be mutually terminated, by whom, when and how much notice should be given by both parties,

---

[1] (HM Government, 2018)

indicating if there are conditions that might be considered breach of contract.

- Invoice and payment
  - Invoicing for services

    State how frequently an invoice should be submitted, what it should include (*invoice number, date, trading or business names, any business or company registration numbers, address*) and what it should include (*activity, dates, fees, expenses and travel as per the engagement*), indicating that if the taxpayer is VAT-registered, then VAT and the VAT registration number need to be added.

    State how other work should be invoiced, if it is additional to the engagement undertaken.

  - Payment for services

    State the date that payments are processed, indicating due date, payment method and whether any exceptions to the payment date might be made.

- Indemnity
  - Status

    Describe the basis under which the engagement is classified for tax purposes, indicating whether fees are subject to deduction of tax or not. Also state who is responsible for the payment of income taxes, social insurance and any other liabilities of a statutory nature that may arise.

  - Indemnity

    State that an indemnity is required regarding any penalties, interest, costs, expenses, damages or proceedings arising out of, or in connection with a claim, assessment, or demand in respect of taxes, contributions or liabilities for fees paid gross, without deduction, despite due diligence and confirmation of the teacher's freelance status.

- Insurance and licences
  - Insurance

    Describe what insurance policies cover activities under this engagement and what insurance polices the teacher will be required to have. This might include reference to use of own car or use of public transport for travel between locations, product and third party liability, employer liability and professional indemnity insurance.

○ Licences

Describe the responsibility to obtain an appropriate and valid licence for copying, burning, or transferring music from vinyl, CD, MP3 or any other commercially produced audio or audio-visual product onto a digital format such as a phone, tablet, MP3 player, flash drive, or laptop for use in the classes.

● Jurisdiction

Describe the jurisdiction under which the agreement will be governed.

The next chapter looks at the use of volunteers in a business.

USING VOLUNTEERS

Some businesses will use volunteers. These can vary from students 16+ in further or higher education to parents and carers helping with open days, school shows, event registrations and selling merchandise.

Volunteers are not paid for their time, but may be given money to cover expenses. This is usually limited to food, drink, travel or any equipment you need to buy for them.

Businesses need to be wary of creating an "employee" out of a volunteer. This can be created by using contractual language or creating mutual obligations rather than reasonable expectations or by providing consideration or money that can be regarded as a payment, reward or benefit-in-kind rather than a payment to cover expenses.[1]

Volunteers invariably come into contact with the same customers as paid employees and freelancers. Employees and freelancers are bound by their Employee handbook, Codes of Professional Practice and Conduct and school rules and regulations, and undergo inductions. Parents and carers may have signed up to their own Code of Customer Behaviour and students to their own Rules and Regulations.

It makes sense for businesses to keep appropriate boundaries between their paid staff and their volunteers, but to ensure that they are valued and treated equally, fairly and consistently.

This chapter discusses the advantages of having a Volunteer Policy.

Volunteer Policy

A Volunteer Policy or Code of Conduct sets out an established framework

---

[1] (HM Government, 2018)

of good practice for businesses that use volunteers in their activities. It helps define the role of volunteers within the organisation and how they can expect to be treated.

The advantages of having a Volunteer Policy are that it can help to:

✓ Demonstrate a commitment to volunteers

✓ Ensure consistent treatment to volunteers

✓ Provide certainty and security to volunteers

✓ Ensure all staff understand the use and role of volunteers

If your business considers using volunteers, you need to give as much attention to them as employing staff and contracting freelancers when applying the same processes of recruitment, selection, induction, training and supervision. A Volunteer Policy should set out the policies applicable to volunteers in the business, and should be shared with employees and volunteers. Consider how best to involve them in your business, consult with your team. Ensure that any policy reflects the size and nature of your business, a proportionate level of formality.

It should include:

✓ Recruitment of volunteers

✓ Role and limitations

✓ Equality and Diversity

✓ Induction and training

✓ Expenses

✓ Supervision and support

✓ Health and Safety

✓ Safeguarding young people and vulnerable people

✓ Privacy statement, confidentiality and privacy

✓ Photography, videos, images and use of social media

✓ Problem solving and complaint procedures for volunteers

✓ Review date

Volunteer Agreements

A businesses can also use Volunteer Agreements to set out both the commitment to its volunteers and what it hopes for from its volunteers.

A volunteer might expect to be:

✓ Provided with induction and training

✓ Supported by an employee, supervisor, manager or owner

✓ Treated in line with any equal opportunity policy

✓ Reimbursed for out-of-pocket expenses

✓ Protected by insurance

✓ Working in a good health and safety environment

A business might require a volunteer to:

✓ Agree to the aims and objectives of the business

✓ Be accountable for their actions

✓ Follow policies and procedures relevant to the role and place within the business

✓ Familiarise themselves with the Volunteer Policy

✓ Meet agreed expectations around the role

As with all types of agreement, appropriate professional advice should be taken.

CHAPTER 18

EXPANDING

KEY POINTS

Assessing your readiness   Sources of growth, retention rates, sustainability, resources
Case Study 2:   Administration   Staffing   Volumes   Operational costs   Owner earnings
Cost structure   Cash flow   Breaking-even   By unit and by revenue   Approaches to expansion

Growth happens differently for every business. For dance schools, growth can occur by attracting more customers to existing classes, providing additional services, or alternatively opening new locations or branches and reaching new customers.

The previous chapters have explored many ideas that can be useful not only for a new business but also one that plans to restructure or expand.

In *Chapter 7: Costing Your Business*, Case Study 1 was used to cost a business. This chapter looks at some of the issues to consider when expanding an existing dance school, and a second Case Study will be used to illustrate how expansion can change your cost basis and break-even. The principles illustrated can be applied to other types of business.

Assessing your readiness

You should consider some key points before deciding to expand your business. The list is not necessarily comprehensive but serves as a reference.

Sources of growth

Where will your growth come from? Will sources for growth (*e.g.*, new dance genre, additional classes, a new branch) support your business strengths and expand or open up opportunities?

You should assess the pros and cons of each source, its cost to your existing business in time and money, and whether there is a ready-made customer base for the expansion. Can you reap economies of scale from expansion?

As your class enrolment expands, you should be able to enjoy cost advantages because the average cost per class, or student, should fall and profitability increases. If costs rise, ensure that your projections of future earnings are realistic.

Retention rates

Customers are your most valuable assets, retaining them can be difficult. You need to build a long-term customer base.

 If a student starts with Pre-school classes and is a promising dancer, you could realistically expect the student to be still with you, aged 16 or 17.

Work out a student retention rate by taking the number of students in your dance school last year, and how many you have today:

$$\frac{\text{No. of students enrolled today}}{\text{No. of students enrolled last year}} \times 100 = \% \text{ Retention rate}$$

This is a relatively simple approach as it is more a reflection of a growth in numbers.

You can refine the equation by using the number of students who transfer from Year 1 to Year 2, to Year 3, etc., as the base; or the number of new students who enrol at the beginning of each academic year or term; or your conversion rate from taster classes to actual enrolment. The more statistics you keep, the more you will be able to drill down and get a better feel for how your dance school is doing operationally and financially.

Whichever base you are using, if you are standing still or growing, the percentage (%) rate should be 100 or more. However, if it is less than 100% then you may need to look at some of these issues:

Dance genre syllabus

    ✓ Are classes challenging?

    ✓ How often does content change?

    ✓ Is the class music stimulating?

    ✓ Is the genre challenging?

Class scheduling

    ✓ Is scheduling convenient for students, parents and carers?

    ✓ Are classes paired or convenient for multiple class choice?

✓ Are classes of the right length?

✓ Are classes frequent enough?

✓ Are classes overcrowded?

Teaching

✓ Can you tell if the teaching is satisfactory?

✓ Are you meeting internal outcomes?

✓ Are your students motivated?

✓ Is there a degree of difficulty?

✓ Do your parents and carers receive feedback?

✓ Do you have a high turnover of staff?

Customer care

✓ Is your dance school a welcoming organisation?

✓ Is the location and area welcoming and accessible?

✓ Are your studios warm and inviting?

✓ Do your students feel part of the school?

✓ Do your parents and carers feel part of the school?

✓ Do you have many complaints?

✓ How do you respond to complaints?

Recruitment

✓ Do you know why students join?

✓ Are you tracking attendance?

✓ Do you have a high turnover of students?

✓ Do you know why students drop out?

Communication

✓ How effective is your communication?

✓ Do you allow feedback?

✓ Do you publish the results of surveys?

Sustainability

Are you able to finance your expansion and sustain it? Expansion can come at an increased cost for a period before profits catch up. Your existing cash flow has to be in good shape and must be able to tide you through if expansion takes longer than expected.

Resources

As when starting a business, it is important to have a Business Plan for expanding. When and how you grow should form part of your business strategy – the right people, skills and resources will support your new business growth. Will your existing business be affected by the expansion? Can your existing employees, processes and resources cope with expansion?

Expect a change in the role you play. Are you willing to play a less hands-on role? You may begin to work with new staff, leaving less time for your current operations and have to delegate responsibilities to others. You should be open to new ways of doing things especially if new partners join you. You may need to spend more time getting to know customers that you no longer have direct contact with through your classes. Your team will need more support from you.

Expansion involves additional risk and pressure, and you should try not to jeopardise your existing business. You should take a slow, steady, incremental approach to expansion. Start with a strong foundation to build your business upon, undertake sound planning and set realistic goals:

○ **Strategies**

Examine your goals, main activities and resources of your business to ensure they are still relevant for future success.

○ **Build your team**

Teamwork is essential no matter what kind of business you run. You need a shared ethos. Strong teams not only drive profits, they can motivate employees to work, learn and grow with your business.

○ **Business processes**

Good business processes can keep an operation streamlined and cost-efficient while undergoing change.

○ **Branding and marketing**

Branding and marketing can be crucial to the success of a business. While *marketing* sells a brand, *branding* presents the package that is a business. Ensure that your branding and marketing have been working, and consider whether they need to be updated.

Case Study 2: Expansion[1]

You have been running *XYZDanz* for a number of years and wish to expand the school by offering other dance genres, while at the same time stepping back from day-to-day teaching. You do not anticipate any change in your self-employment status but the office will move to the studio.

You have used the following facts and assumptions for the budget and Business Plan:

Administration

- Rental: Two studios, two office spaces, continuing use of common areas such as changing rooms, central reception, and heating and lighting.
- Term: Annual rental for whole space.
- Maintenance: Responsible for the studios and common areas.
- Office: Managing your business from the studio.
- Travel: Travelling expenses to and from the studio by the freelance staff.

You have now reached your original target for classes and volume, and plan to double your existing timetable.

- Dance genre: Ballet, Other genre (to be decided) plus Pilates and Yoga
- Studio day: Monday to Friday – 6 hours each day, Saturday – 7 hours
- Term time: 3 terms of 12-weeks duration
- Studios: Two

  Per studio:
- Classes: Monday to Friday 4 classes each day; Saturday – 5 classes
- Class duration: Between 45–75 minutes
- Class size: Average of 15 per class
- Teaching day: Monday to Friday – 4 hours each day; Saturday – 5 hours

---

[1] As with Case Study 1, some of the costs, volumes, assumptions, tax treatment or benefits may not always apply to everyone's personal situation, or the jurisdiction in which a business operates. Income and costs are illustrative only and no reliance should be made on hourly rates quoted. £ Sterling is used as the currency unit (CU) but the figures can be converted to any appropriate currency unit. Rounding differences may occur in the tables and examples.

Staffing

Although you have decided to step back from regular teaching to take on more administrative duties, you will continue to teach the adult and older learners. *XYZDanz* will employ a full-time teacher to teach ballet from Pre-school to Level 8 and undertake some administration. Freelancers will be contracted to teach the other dance genre, Yoga and Pilates.

There will be 50 hours of teaching a week:

	Level	Age	Total time
2 classes of 45 mins.	Pre-School	3–4	1.50
4 classes of 45 mins.	Pre-Primary	5	3.00
4 classes of 45 mins.	Primary	6	3.00
4 classes of 1 hour	Level 1	7	4.00
4 classes of 1 hour	Level 2	8	4.00
4 classes of 1 hour	Level 3	9	4.00
4 classes of 1 hour	Level 4	10	4.00
4 classes of 1 hour	Level 5	11	4.00
4 classes of 1¼ hours	Level 6	13	5.00
4 classes of 1¼ hours	Level 7	15	5.00
4 classes of 1¼ hours	Level 8	17	5.00
2 classes of 45 mins.	Pilates		1.50
1 class of 1 hour	Yoga		1.00
3 classes of 1 hour	Adult		3.00
2 classes of 1 hour	Older Learners	55+	2.00
50 classes			50 hours

Taught by:

		Monday–Friday	Saturday	Total hours
Owner	Adult	2	3	5
Teacher (employee)	Ballet	19	3	22
Teachers (freelance)	Other genre	17	3	20
Teachers (freelance)	Pilates / Yoga	2	1	3
		40	**10**	**50**

You will hire another assistant. Both assistants will share the task of opening the studios; registering students on arrival; dealing with problems on site; ensuring that students leave safely; closing the studios, and undertaking other administrative duties as well as assisting in the studio when needed.

You will continue to use recorded music in your classes and contract musicians to play for your classes appropriate to the genre once a term.

Volumes

With the expansion, there will be 1,800 hours a year (g), based on 50 hours of classes per week over a 36-week period:

Number of classes per week:	Hours	
Length of each class	1	
Monday–Friday – 5 days × 4 hours × 2 studios per day	40	(a)
Saturday – 1 day × 5 hours × 2 studios per day	10	(b)
Total hours per week (a + b)	50	(c)

This can be summarised as:

	Units	
Number of terms	3	(d)
Number of weeks per term	12	(e)
Number of weeks per year (d × e)	36	(f)
Number of hours per year (c × f)	1,800	(g)
Number of students per class	15	

Operational costs

XYZDanz has been operating successfully at the budget levels envisaged in Case Study 1 and in Year 3 of the cash flow. Case Study 2 will treat these as the base for the actual operating income and costs, to which will be added any additions or changes in income and costs that can be expected from the expansion plans.

● **Fixed costs** will increase with the employment of a ballet teacher, the change to a fixed annual rent and some anticipated changes in costs. The initial loan will have been paid off.

Table 18.1 Case Study 2: Fixed costs

	Actual £	Addition or change £	Revised costs £
Studio and office lease	–	60,000	60,000
Teacher's salary	–	30,000	30,000
Social insurance costs (employer contribution)	–	3,000	3,000
Pension costs (employer contribution)	–	900	900
Class assistants' salaries	16,200	16,200	32,400
Social insurance costs (employer contribution)	1,620	1,620	3,240
Pension costs (employer contribution)	480	480	960
Teaching materials	500	500	1,000
Costumes and uniform	300	300	600
Class props	200	200	400
Subscriptions and journals	200	–	200
Travel costs (freelancers)	700	–	700
Accountancy	400	600	1,000
Insurance	450	550	1,000
Telephone fixed line and broadband	400	100	500
Systems software subscription and fees	800	–	800
Affiliation subscription and training courses	500	500	1,000
Office costs (studio)	600	–	600
Loan interest (£59 × 12)	708	(708)	–
Miscellaneous	600	300	900
Total fixed costs	**£24,658**	**£114,542**	**£139,200**

- **Semi-fixed costs** will reduce as the rent has become a fixed cost, but there are some anticipated increases.

- **Variable costs** will decrease from the reduction in your notional teaching time, but will increase due to your notional administrative time, contracting freelance teachers, musician costs for the additional dance genres, and a provision in case your employee teacher falls ill and is unable to carry out either teaching or administration.

Table 18.2 Case Study 2: Semi-fixed costs

	Actual	Addition or change	Revised costs
	£	£	£
Studio and office rental	25,308	(25,308)	–
Maintenance and repair	400	200	600
Advertising, promotion and marketing	2,000	1,500	3,500
Printing, postage and stationery	500	700	1,200
Mobile costs and phone calls	400	100	500
Bank and credit card (cc) charges	500	250	750
Sundry expenses	392	308	700
Total semi-fixed costs	**£29,500**	**£(22,250)**	**£7,250**

Table 18.3 Case Study 2: Variable costs

	Actual	Addition or change	Revised costs
	£	£	£
Owner-teacher cost	24,300	(19,440)	4,860
Administrative time	9,720	10,080	19,800
Teacher replacement cost (employee)	–	7,128	7,128
Class assistant replacement cost (employee)	6,000	–	6,000
Freelance teacher cost	–	22,356	22,356
Freelance musician cost	1,898	1,669	3,567
Total variable costs	**£41,918**	**£21,793**	**£63,711**

○ **Owner-teacher cost**: Your revised owner-teacher cost is costed at £4,860 as your teaching will be cut to 5 hours a week, and any remaining time will be spent running the business:

Monday–Friday, Saturday – 5 days × 1 hour	5	(a)
Number of terms	3	(b)
Number of weeks per term	12	(c)
Total hours in year (a × b × c)	180	(d)
Total owner-teacher cost – 180 hours × £27	£4,860	

🔆 It can be good practice to include the teaching cost of the owner in a budget, as this effectively includes a freelance "replacement" cost if sickness interferes or circumstances change.

○ **Administrative time:** You and your employee teacher will undertake at least 35 hours per week in administration. This is the equivalent of a full-time administrative employee. You have decided that you should budget an additional £19,800 (£18,000 plus 10% social insurance and pension costs).

🔆 It can be good practice to include the administrative cost of the owner as well as the employee in the calculations, as this is effectively an administration "replacement" cost if sickness interferes or circumstances change.

○ **Employee teacher replacement cost:** You will employ a full-time teacher to cover your former teaching time. The teacher will teach the ballet stream Monday to Saturday, 22 hours per week. As a full-time employee, the teacher will also undertake an additional 23 hours of administrative and planning time. The total salary costs are included in fixed costs.

If your employee teacher fell sick, they would be entitled to be paid and you would have to find a replacement. This would be an additional cost. *XYZDanz* pays a freelance rate of £27 per hour, an assumed median rate at the time of publication, for a (replacement) teacher:

Monday–Friday – 19 hours	19	(a)
Saturday – 3 hours	3	(b)
Total hours per week (a + b)	22	(c)
Number of terms	1	(d)
Number of weeks per term	12	(e)
Total hours in term (c × d × e)	264	(f)
Teacher (replacement) cost – 264 hours × £27	£7,128	

🔆 It can be prudent to build in a contingency in case the employee teacher falls sick and *XYZDanz* has to contract a freelancer to cover.

🔆 Budget for one term's costs as it can be easier to recruit a replacement for a longer period.

○ **Employee class assistant replacement cost:** Two class assistants will assist in some of the classes, undertake registration and administration. Both will work 25 hours per week. The assistants are employees and a fixed cost and if either of them fell sick, they would be entitled to be paid and you would have to find a replacement.

XYZDanz will pay a casual rate of £20 per hour (£18 per hour plus 10% in additional employer costs for social insurance and pension costs) for a (replacement) assistant, an assumed median rate at the time of publication:

Monday–Friday – 5 days × 4 hours	20	(a)
Saturday – 1 day × 5 hours	5	(b)
Total hours per week (a + b)	25	(c)
Number of terms	1	(d)
Number of weeks per term	12	(e)
Total hours in year (c × d × e)	300	(f)
Assistant (replacement) cost – 300 hours × £20	£6,000	

- It can be prudent to build in a contingency in case an assistant fell sick.

- The contingency could be based on one assistant and one term's cost, as it can be easier to recruit a replacement for a longer period.

○ **Freelance teachers cost:** Freelance teachers are paid £27 per hour, an assumed median rate at the time of publication. They are contracted 19 hours between Monday and Friday and 4 hours on Saturday. There are no additional payroll costs for the teachers as they are self-employed:

Monday–Friday – 19 hours	19	(a)
Saturday – 4 hours	4	(b)
Total hours per week (a + b)	23	(c)
Number of terms	3	(d)
Number of weeks per term	12	(e)
Total hours in year (c × d × e)	828	(f)
Total freelance cost – 828 hours × £27	£22,356	

○ **Freelance musicians cost:** You will provide live accompaniment in class (excluding Yoga and Pilates) for one week per term. Accompanists can vary from pianists, to drum players, to string, depending on the class and genre. You pay £23 per hour, an assumed median rate at the time of publication. Musicians can incur an additional 10% in social insurance and pension costs:

Monday–Friday – 38 hours	38	(a)
Saturday – 9 hours	9	(b)
Total hours (a + b)	47	(c)
Number of terms	3	(d)
Total hours in year (c × d)	141	(e)
Total musician cost – 141 hours × £25.30[2]	£3,567	

Owner earnings and profit

When starting out, you built in an element of earnings for yourself by budgeting for your own teaching and administrative time, as well as a replacement assistant. In both of these cases, you were just being prudent because if you or the assistant fell sick this contingency would have been used.

This provision was substantial as you were undertaking the teaching yourself. You have decided to step back and employ a teacher who will take on your teaching commitments and share the administration with you, such as planning, timetabling, freelance resourcing, trouble-shooting, planning for other activities and making sure the fees are collected.

This will change the nature of your involvement in the business. You will be more involved with administration, success and growth of the business. With this change, your earnings from your teaching will be minimal and you will have to rely on the profits from the business to provide you with a salary.

Your total earnings, including notional costs and profits, however could increase from £44,020 to potentially £51,788, because of the increased profit and an assumption that you would replace the employed teacher when sick, either teaching or undertaking more administrative work:

	Actual	Revised costs
	£	£
Owner-teacher cost	24,300	4,860
Administrative time	9,720	19,800
Employee teacher replacement cost	–	7,128
Profits	10,000	20,000
Earnings (salary) and profit	**£44,020**	**£51,788**

[2] includes 10% additional cost on the hourly rate of £23

Cost structure

You have now calculated the fixed, semi-fixed and variable costs, and your "salary". There has been a shift to fixed costs, which will make it more critical that your revised projections are met. Your expansion plans have added a further £114,085 to costs, and there has been a change in the cost structure of *XYZDanz* from the profile shown in Case Study 1:

Table 18.4: Case Study 2: Summary of costs

	Actual	Addition or change	Revised costs
	£	£	£
Fixed costs	24,658	114,542	139,200
Semi-fixed costs	29,500	(22,250)	7,250
Variable costs	41,918	21,793	63,711
Total costs	**£96,076**	**£114,085**	**£210,161**

Although the hourly cost per class has only risen from £123.04 to £127.86 (1,800 hours), an increase of 3.82% ([£127.86 ÷ £123.04] − 1 = .0382%), there has been a fundamental shift in the financial profile:

Table 18.5: Case Study 2: Revised financial profile

	Original cost model			Revised cost model		
	£	Hours	£	£	Hours	£
			Per hour			Per hour
Fixed costs	24,658	900	27.40	139,200	1,800	77.33
Semi-fixed costs	29,500	900	32.77	7,250	1,800	4.03
Variable costs	7,898	900	8.78	31,923	1,800	17.73
Owner-teacher time	34,020	900	37.80	31,788	1,800	17.66
Profit element	14,656	900	16.28	20,000	1,800	11.11
Total costs	**£110,732**		**£123.04**	**£230,161**		**£127.86**
Per student		15	**£8.20**		15	**£8.52**

There has been an approximate 35% increase in hourly fixed and semi-fixed costs. As can be seen from the following break-even analysis, the BEP has deteriorated rather than improved. It has become more critical that the business can generate sufficient income to cover the increase in fixed costs. In Case Study 1 the BEP for turnover per term was £19,432, for Case Study 2 it has risen to £56,678.

The overall 3.9% increase in hourly costs can easily be covered by an increase in fees to maintain profit margins. The fee per student will increase from £8.20 to £8.52 before consumption tax. It is likely however that your liability to consumption tax will change if you had been previously able to take advantage of the Tribunal Case cited earlier in *Chapter 11: Paying Taxes*.

Cash flow

Case Study 2 is intended to show how the cost structure can change. This can affect your cash flow projection; for example, if there are more fixed costs going out per month, then your cash flow funding requirement can change from that shown in Case Study 1. You can work out whether your expansion plans are self-financing or whether short-term funding is required and when, by using the method outlined in *Chapter 9: Analysing Cash Flow*.

Breaking-even

All the the BEPs will have increased or deteriorated rather than improved or become more achievable because fixed costs have increased due to the employment of a teacher and a fixed annual rent. How they compare:

Break-even by gross profit margin

Using gross profit margin, you will achieve your annual BEP with sales of £170,034. The BEP has increased to 74% from 53% because your fixed costs are higher:

- Gross profit = sales – variable cost

  Gross profit % margin = gross profit ÷ sales × 100

  Break-even point by sales = (fixed cost ÷ gross profit % margin) ×100
- Gross profit = (£230,161 – £31,923) = £198,238

  Gross profit % margin = £198,328 ÷ £230,161 × 100 = 86.13%

  Break-even point = £146,450 ÷ 86.13% ×100 = £170,034

Break-even by revenue per school term or weeks

Break-even point per term = £170,034 ÷ 3 = **£56,678** (Case Study 1: **£19,432**)
Break-even point per week = £170,034 ÷ 36 = £4,722 (Case Study 1: £1,619)

Break-even by unit

Analysing the expansion plan:

○ Attendance profile (per week):

Number of classes per week	50	
Number of weeks per term	12	
Number of classes per term	600	(a)
Average number per class	15	
Number of students per week[3]	750	(b)

○ Fixed and semi-fixed cost profile (per term):

Fixed costs	£139,200	
Semi-fixed costs	£7,250	
Total fixed and semi-fixed costs	£146,450	
Per term (÷3)	£48,816	(c)

○ Fees per class and per student (per term):

Total fees received (3 terms)	£230,161	
Fees per term	£76,720	(d)
Budgeted no. of classes per term (a)	600	
Average fee per class per term (d) ÷ (a)	£127.86	(e)
Budgeted no. of students per term (b)	750	
Average fee per student per term (d) ÷ (b)	£102.29	(f)

○ Variable costs per class and per student (per term):

Variable costs (3 terms) (excluding notional costs)	£31,923	
Variable costs per term	£10,641	(g)
Budgeted no. of classes per term (a)	600	
Variable cost per class per term (g) ÷ (a)	£17.74	(h)
Budgeted no. of students per term (b)	750	
Variable cost per student per term (g) ÷ (b)	£14.19	(i)

[3] Pupil roll can include the same pupil taking more than one class

○ Per class

Break-even point per class (units) = fixed cost ÷ (sales price − variable cost)
Break-even point per class (units) =   (c)   ÷ ((e)   −   (h)   )

Break-even point per class = £48,816 ÷ £110.12 (£127.86 − £17.74)
Break-even point per class = 443 classes (Case Study 1: 158 classes)

○ Per student

Break-even point per student (units) = fixed cost ÷ (sales price − variable cost)
Break-even point per student (units) =   (c)   ÷ ((f)   −   (i)   )

Break-even point per student = £48,816 ÷ £88.10 (£102.29 − £14.19)
Break-even point per student = 554 students (Case Study 1: 197 students)

Break-even by unit revenue per class or per student

Break-even point in costs/revenue = the break-even point in units × sales price
Break-even point in revenue = the break-even point per class × sales price

Break-even point by class revenue per term = 443 × £127.86 = £56,641
(Case Study 1: £19,440)
Break-even point by student revenue per term = 554 × £102.29 = £56,668
(Case Study 1: £19,393)

Approaches to expansion

As discussed previously, the BEP illustrates the number of classes (with 15 in each class or averaged across all classes) that you need to hold, the number of students that you need to attract, or revenues per week or term to cover your fixed and semi-fixed costs.

As can be seen from Case Study 2, expanding can possibly overstretch a business. Case Study 2 illustrates that earnings have not improved significantly, and the change in cost structure to fixed costs has raised the risk, as the business has to bring in more revenue to cover those costs week after week.

Your decision to withdraw from teaching has added a cost of £30,000+. You might want to consider expanding in a different way. You could take a phased approach. Take on the additional studios and offer the additional dance genre, but continue teaching yourself.

This will improve cash flow because fixed costs will be reduced by £30,000; this cost will become a notional cost and the BEPs are lowered.

Alternatively rather than employ a teacher, take on freelance staff to cover all the classes. This may involve more administration, but it provides opportunities to reduce cost by cancelling classes.

Alternatively, you could plan additional activities and thereby additional revenue outside term time using the spare studio capacity, because the lease is for 52 weeks a year. You could consider rentals to community groups; scheduling Yoga and Pilates classes all year round for adults and older learners; holding workshops and other events during the holiday period; or extending the term time to 40 weeks.

These additional activities can be treated as separate projects for budgeting purposes.

When you are planning expansion you might wish to explore all the options available to you and calculate "What if" scenarios before settling on the plan you feel will work. One of those "What if" scenarios could be to buy your own premises. The next chapter explores the issues behind buying and selling an existing business.

CHAPTER 19

BUYING (OR SELLING) A BUSINESS

KEY POINTS

Considerations when buying, selling, closing down   Setting a price   Definition of value
Elements of valuation   Valuation techniques   Calculating value   Multiple of earnings
Multiple of turnover   Students on the register   Negotiation techniques   Franchises

Dance businesses are often available for sale. Owners who are looking to sell can use a variety of methods:

✓ Word of mouth

✓ National press – businesses for sale

✓ Dance press – *e.g.,* Dancing Times, Dance Australia, Dance International, Dance, Dance Europe

✓ Dance Awarding Organisation networks – *e.g.,* Royal Academy of Dance's JobSearch, IDTA classifieds.

✓ Numerous websites – *e.g.,* Dance Teachers Network, NDTA

In the past, dance schools have occasionally been given to a favoured student, or retiring owners have simply closed their schools. In such cases, no financial transactions have arisen because of the belief that there was no value attached to the business.

The chapter explores the issues behind buying or selling a business.

Considerations, when buying

The prospective business owner might consider it easier to buy an existing business rather than set one up from scratch. In either case, you will still be subject to the same pressures, having to build up by yourself or having to work to pay for somebody else's success.

If you were starting your own business, you would go through the steps discussed in earlier chapters. Your Business Plan would have provided you with the blueprint for establishing a new business. Buying a business should be no different. You could write your Business Plan from the perspective of buying an existing business and identify within the plan the ideal size, market, best location, desired turnover, operational structure, the level of profitability, and the sum you are prepared to pay.

You can use this as the blueprint for identifying prospective businesses for sale. It is always advisable to seek professional help, as there are many questions that a prospective buyer can ask. You should commission a comprehensive appraisal of the business to establish its assets and liabilities and evaluate its commercial potential. This is known as due diligence. An accountancy or legal firm should be able to help with this. A mentor from the dance world should be able to help you appraise the business itself.

There will be many varied reasons why an owner wishes to sell, and when buying a business you need to "flush out" any reasons that might not be instantly obvious. The business may not be very profitable and the Financial Statements should be able to tell you this. You should obtain at least three years' accounts, as you need to determine if a downturn happened. Ask for accounts from earlier years if you feel a downturn occurred over a longer period; be wary if there are no formal accounts available. Sole traders and partnerships do not always need to have formal accounts prepared; however, a successful and confident business should have had them prepared by their advisers.

Reasons for sale could include:

- ✓ Retirement
- ✓ Moving away
- ✓ Family reasons
- ✓ Ill health or passed away
- ✓ Change of career
- ✓ Raising a family
- ✓ Business too big to manage
- ✓ Falling volumes
- ✓ Increased regulation
- ✓ Increased competition
- ✓ Negligence or other personal liability claim
- ✓ Losing money

Reasons for losing money could include:

- ✓ Standards have dropped
- ✓ Owner has lost focus

- ✓ Frequent changes in staff
- ✓ Local competition has increased
- ✓ Single product or dance genre
- ✓ Business hasn't kept up with the times
- ✓ Premises are tired
- ✓ Business has been sold frequently
- ✓ Demographics of catchment area has shrunk
- ✓ Changing market conditions
- ✓ Fees haven't kept pace with costs
- ✓ Bad debts or slow payees

You should compare the actual costs of the business you are considering purchasing to those that you would expect to incur. This will give you an insight into whether the business has been operating without costs such as advertising, insurance, music licences, web presence, etc., and how much the existing profitability might be affected by the type of costs you anticipate. This can affect the price you are prepared to pay.

Due diligence will answer many questions, but among them, find out:

- ✓ Why is the business being sold?

Structure

- ✓ What is the structure of the business – sole trader, partnership, company?
- ✓ How personal is the business?
- ✓ Is the owner a key person?
- ✓ How long has the business been in existence?
- ✓ Is there a business name?
- ✓ Is the name protected?
- ✓ How long has the business been in existence?
- ✓ Are there any legal concerns?

Finances

- ✓ What do the financial statements tell you?
- ✓ Is it a going concern?
- ✓ What is being sold – name, assets, receivables and payables (debtors and creditors)?

✓ How important is the business name – goodwill?

✓ Will the departure of the owner affect the business?

✓ What is the condition of any assets for sale?

✓ What receivables are due?

✓ What is the customer payment pattern?

✓ What payables are due?

✓ What is the credit history?

✓ Will suppliers renew on similar or better terms?

✓ What is the policy on fees?

✓ When was the last price increase?

✓ Why are some types of cost or expenditure missing?

✓ Has anything been paid by third parties and not recorded?

✓ Are there any off-balance sheet liabilities?

Services

✓ What dance genres are taught?

✓ Is the business affiliated to a particular Dance Awarding Organisation?

✓ How many students are enrolled?

✓ What are the class sizes?

✓ What makes this business different from others?

✓ Is turnover, or student numbers, in decline and, if so, why?

✓ Is turnover, or student numbers, rising and, if so, why?

✓ What is the competition?

✓ Is there a business brochure or other literature?

✓ Are there terms of agreement between the business and individual customers?

✓ What might happen if the fees are raised?

✓ Where do the majority of students come from, and why do they come?

✓ Do all students pay fees?

Staffing

✓ How many teachers are there?

✓ Are they employed or freelance?

✓ Will key staff leave or remain with a new owner?

✓ What type of contracts are staff on?

✓ Are volunteers used?

✓ How much reliance is on volunteers?

✓ Are there any redundancy or transfer issues to consider?

Premises

✓ Are the premises rented or owned?

✓ Is there more than one location?

✓ Are the premises fit-for-purpose?

✓ Are they big enough for the customer base?

✓ What is the remaining period of any property rental or agreement?

✓ Is there a break clause in any agreement?

✓ What is the condition of the premises like?

✓ Who is responsible for the maintenance?

✓ How often are they maintained?

✓ Are there development plans or planning/zoning laws that might affect the area?

✓ What is the annual business or property tax?

✓ What is the annual insurance premium?

✓ Has a valuation been made?

Considerations, when selling

A seller might wish to consider the following to ensure that a sale goes through:

✓ Timing of sale

✓ Assumption of receivables and payables (debtors and creditors)

✓ Staying on as a consultant

✓ Selling the business name

✓ Assignment of leases and agreements

✓ Providing a non-compete guarantee

✓ Allowing purchase by instalment

✓ Tax implications

✓ Press release

Considerations, when closing down

If an owner wishes to close down a business, consideration might be given to:

- ✓ Timing of closure
- ✓ Employee redundancies
- ✓ Receivables and payables (debtors and creditors)
- ✓ Contract terms
- ✓ Tax implications
- ✓ Future of customer base
- ✓ Press release

Setting a price

The right price for any business is subjective. It comes down to what the buyer is prepared to pay and what the seller is prepared to accept. In the following paragraphs, the definition of value, and the methods you could use to set a purchase price are explored.

Definition of value[1]

The concept of value has always been difficult to define because it must, of necessity, be subjective. Quite frequently, "value" is automatically equated with cost or monetary equivalent. This is not always correct. There are at least four types of value:

- ○ Use value
- ○ Exchange value
- ○ Esteem value
- ○ Cost value

For example, water has a low cost value but its use value is extremely high. In times of drought its exchange value and cost value increase rapidly; conversely, in times of plenty, the reverse happens.

Can these values apply to dance schools?

There is often confusion between cost and value. The cost of an item can be increased without adding a penny to its use value. Similar difficulties exist when trying to create a single basis by which a business, in monetary terms, can be valued.

[1] (Royal Academy of Dance, 2015)

Elements of valuation

All kinds of businesses are bought and sold for money, including dance schools. The following four elements should be considered in any valuation:

● Goodwill value

The goodwill element of any business valuation is essentially dependent on the profitability of the business and the degree of certainty that such profits will continue in the future.

The Royal Institution of Chartered Surveyors, a professional body that accredits professionals within the land, property, construction and infrastructure sectors worldwide, defines goodwill as "the estimated amount for which an asset should be exchanged on the date of valuation, between a willing buyer and a willing seller, in an arm's length transaction after proper marketing wherein the parties have acted knowledgeably, prudently and without compulsion".

The estimated amount or value can be derived in various ways, for example, from the length of time that the school has been in operation, the reputation of the seller and the business name, or even the term fees (see below).

● Property value

It is important to distinguish between a dance school which includes a property interest, and one that does not. As will be appreciated, many schools have long-standing arrangements with other schools and local organisations. However, in terms of property rights, the arrangement is often a simple lease, which may be terminated by the property owner at short notice. The notice and lease periods are also factors that can hold back the goodwill value of the business. It is a matter of judgement over the relative worth of one lease in comparison with another.

When a dance school has a legal interest in property, whether freehold or leasehold, then a greater degree of certainty (and hence value) is introduced into the goodwill element. Anyone purchasing a leasehold or freehold property interest will need guidance from professional advisers, such as a solicitor practising commercial law and a chartered surveyor, to value the property.

● Contents value

Fixtures and fittings have a value, which needs to be taken into account. It would be fairest to approach this from the point of view of a written down value (WDV), which is fairly reflected by an annual figure for depreciation. However, not all assets depreciate at the same rate, so care should be taken to consider the future useful life of each item and to balance this against the current replacement cost.

● Stock value

It is traditional to set the value of any stock, such as uniforms, portable barres, music libraries, etc., on the day of exchange, so that an accurate inventory can be taken. Damaged or out-of-date stock should not be included.

Valuation techniques

The purpose and the objective of the valuation will influence both the choice of technique and the final figure. Nevertheless, the basic approach to valuation can be by reference to two bases: (1) what the business owns in assets, or (2) what the business creates in earnings.

In both cases, a factor that underpins the valuation of a dance school (or any business) is the alternative option available to the prospective buyer, *e.g.,* being able to start up a new business instead. Start-ups are inherently more uncertain and, indeed, may incur losses in the early years. Therefore, buying an existing business can be viewed as being more cost-effective rather than starting anew. You should ensure, however, that the assets you are buying and the price you are paying would generate the revenue and costs you are expecting. Some assets may not be suitable and will have to be replaced, stock might be obsolete, goodwill may be tarnished and the debts may all be bad.

The techniques are discussed only to demonstrate how businesses can be valued:

● Asset basis

Businesses will obtain fixed assets at a price and these will reduce in value over time as they wear out. This consumption of an asset is known as depreciation. Fixed assets will normally have the greatest effect on the overall valuation.

You may wish to buy (or sell) a dance business that owns its own studio and equipment, or has a long-term lease. It may be quite easy to establish the figure for the land and buildings, or long-term lease. Valuing equipment may be more difficult. In this case, reference could be made to replacement cost, reduced by the condition or the number of years expectancy left in the equipment. Some equipment may not be required, so should be disregarded.

● Earning basis

An alternative approach to assessing the value of a business is to assess the "sum it is worth" paying *now* for the future earnings of the business. Companies employ complex mathematical formulas using rates of return and super profits. These would be difficult to apply in the case of a sole trader, and usually a very simple formula can be used:

"n" years × average profits, where "n" is a multiplier

Calculating value

XYZDanz has been operating for three years but the owner has decided to sell for personal reasons. You are an interested buyer. Using the profits from Table 11.5 in *Chapter 11: Paying Taxes*, the profits have been £55,159 (current year) for the year in which the school has been put up for sale, £33,015 for the penultimate year (current year minus 1) and £10,868 for the prior year (current year minus 2).

How might the buyer or seller value the school?

Multiple of earnings

This is one of the more widely used valuation methods. It is based on profits and a multiplier. This is the "n" years × average profits formula where "n" is the multiplier.

Profits are normally adjusted. For larger businesses, profits would normally be re-stated before interest, tax, depreciation and amortisation. For the prospective dance school owner, net profits might have to be adjusted because the profits will be diluted, for example, if:

✓ You will employ a manager or dance teacher to operate the school for you; Or

✓ You identify costs the business should have incurred; Or

✓ You will incur interest on a loan to purchase the business; Or

✓ The additional financial benefit of purchase to you is worth less than the profit

However, average profits can be calculated in a number of ways even before any adjustments.

○ **Value based on the profits of the current year**

XYZDanz has current profits of **£55,159** (adjusted for the earnings of the owner)

○ **Value based on the average profits of the last three years**

XYZDanz has had the following profits profile:

	£
Current year	55,159
Previous year (current year – 1)	33,015
Penultimate year (current year – 2)	10,868
	£99,042
Average profits (£99,042 ÷ 3)	**£33,014**

This is a simple arithmetic mean with each year contributing equally to the average.

○ **Value based on the average weighted profits of the last three years**

	£	x	£
Current year	55,159	3	165,477
Previous year (current year – 1)	33,015	2	66,030
Penultimate year (current year- 2)	10,868	1	10,868
	£99,042	**6**	**£242,375**
Weighted profits (£242,375 ÷ 6)			**£40,396**

This assumes that some figures carry more importance than others. In this case, the average has been weighted in favour of the profits made in the current year, using a diminishing factor of 3, 2 and 1.

○ **Value based on the additional financial benefit to the buyer**

You may be looking at the purchase of a school to enhance earnings. Let us assume you are presently employed as a dance teacher by another school and earn £20,000 before tax. Purchase of XYZDanz would increase your earnings to £55,159 before tax; therefore, the additional financial benefit to you would be **£35,159**.

Multiple of turnover

This is a variation of a method used by businesses that generate regular ongoing revenue from an existing customer base. It simply calculates the value of the business as a multiple of its turnover.

XYZDanz has term fees of **£36,911** (£110,732 ÷ 3).

Number of students on the register

The number of students on the register is a traditional method. XYZDanz has 25 classes of 15 attendees each, in total 375. If 1/3rd of the students take one class only and the remainder two classes, there would be 250 students on the register.

Based on 250 students, the value of each student can be calculated using any of the above bases:

	Based on calculated value	Value per student on register
Latest profits	£55,159	£221
Weighted profits (3 years)	£40,396	£162
Average profits (3 years)	£33,014	£132
Additional benefit	£35,159	£141
Term fees	£36,911	£148

This method could be applied to ensure student retention following the sale. Each student has a potential loss value, which could be applied if students leave within a certain period – because the school had changed hands. This method may however be difficult to apply because there are many reasons why students leave.

An alternative might be to retain the owner as a consultant or include a non-compete clause in the sale contract.

Negotiation techniques

These valuation methods give the buyer and seller and their advisers a point of reference to consider multipliers and adjustments, and from which to negotiate. The multiplier used depends on the industry and the size of the business. Dance schools tend to have relatively small turnovers and so the multiplier will probably be at the lower end, and as a rough guide between 1, 1½ and 2.

The only right price is the price the buyer will pay and the seller will accept.

- Consider what has come out in the due diligence exercise.

- Use the additional benefit argument to your advantage.

- Be realistic about what you end up paying for.

- Consider linking price to future performance, achievement of milestones or by instalment.

- Consider retaining owner to keep goodwill and establish yourself.

Franchises

There are also dance franchises whereby you can buy into a successful brand and have the support of the franchisor behind you.

Franchises have many of the advantages that you might be looking for – your own business, a tried and tested format, advice and support, a recognised brand. The disadvantages can be that you may have to follow the franchisor's artistic vision, pay fees for it, may be limited in expansion, and while successful in your part of the franchise others may not be and the brand and possibly the financial stability of the franchise will suffer, along with you.

It is good idea if you are interested to find out as much as you can about franchises and franchisors. Speak to existing franchisees. There are many regulatory bodies representing the franchise industries and companies, which try to steer potential franchisees through the many opportunities that franchising can offer. The British Franchising Association (BFA), a voluntary self-regulatory body for the franchise sector in the United Kingdom, can provide objective advice and information to prospective franchisees and franchisors.

EPILOGUE

This book has explored issues related to starting out as an employee, employer or self-employed to expanding, selling or buying an expanding business. The issues herein have been intended to provide guidance towards those first steps – into employment, starting your own business, or towards restructuring, expanding or selling an existing business.

While this book has used examples of legislation, policies and procedures from the United Kingdom, it has tried to provide content that is general rather than specific in nature so that it can appeal to students, teachers and professionals wherever they live and work, and so the book is general rather than specific in nature. Where it has been necessary to be specific, the principles can usually be applied elsewhere.

The Appendices include some additional information, which may be of help.

- Appendix 1: Self-employed names as referred to in other countries.
- Appendix 2: Taxpayer identification numbers (TINs) as referred to in other countries.
- Appendix 3: Registries for searching business names.
- Appendix 4: Dance Awarding Organisations that offer graded examinations in dance.

Text marked with a 🔆 is a mixture of hints and tips. As has been said throughout this book, you should always take appropriate professional advice before making any decision and should not merely rely on these and certain general statements made in this book, which may not apply to individual circumstances.

It is not intended to provide you with formal legal, accounting or other professional advice and no such advice has been given in this book.

It is hoped that this book has provided you with an overview of what you need to consider when taking up employment, setting up your own dance business, expanding or selling your present one.

SELF-EMPLOYED NAMES

UK	Sole trader
Australia	Independent contractor
Austria	Eingetragenes Einzelunternehmen (e.U)
Belgium	Eenmanszaak
Brazil	Profissionais Autônomos / Empreendedor Individual
Canada	Sole proprietor (SP)
Chile	Empresa individual de responsabilidad limitada (EIRL)
China	Sole proprietor/独资经营
Cyprus	Sole proprietor
Denmark	Enkeltmandsvirksomhed
France	Auto-entrepreneur
Germany	Eingetragener Einzelunternehmen
Greece	Αυτο μισθωτού εργαζομένου
Guatemala	Trabajadores autónomos
Hong Kong	Sole proprietor
Indonesia	Usaha Dagang (UD)
Ireland	Sole trader
Israel	Atzmai/יאמצע
Italy	Imprenditore
Jamaica	Self-employed
Japan	自営, フリーランス
Luxembourg	Enterprise individuelle
Malaysia	Peniaga Tunggal/Pemilik Tunggal
Malta	Self-employed
Mexico	Pequeña y Mediana Empresa (PYME)
Netherlands	Eenmanszaak
New Zealand	Self-employed/independent contractor
Norway	Enkeltpersonforetak
Peru	Trabajadores por cuenta propia
Philippines	Self-employed
Portugal	Trabalhadores independentes
Singapore	Sole proprietor

South Africa	Sole proprietor
Spain	Trabajadores autónomos
Sri Lanka	Self-employed worker
Sweden	Enskild firma
Switzerland	Einzelunternehmen; raison individuelle; Ditta individuale
Taiwan	Sole proprietor/獨資經營
Thailand	Entrepreneur/เจ้าของกิจการ
Turkey	Şahis firmasi
UAE	Self-employed
USA	Independent contractor

TAXPAYER IDENTIFICATION NUMBERS

UK	Unique Taxpayers Reference/National Insurance Number	UTR/NINO
Australia	Tax File Number	TFN
Austria	Steuern No	Str. No
Belgium	Numéro National	NN
Brazil	Cadastro de Contribuintes Mobiliarios/ Cadastro de Pessoa Fisica	CCM/CPF
Canada	Social Insurance Number	SIN
Chile	Rol Único Nacional	RUN
China	Resident Identity Card Number/ 居民身份证号码	ID
Cyprus	Tax Identification Code	TIC
Denmark	Civil Registration Number/Centrale Personregister	CPR
France	Numéro d'inscription au répertoire	NIR
Germany	Steuerliche Identifikationsnummer	Steuer-IdNr
Greece	Tax Identity Number/Αριθμός Φορολογικού Μητρώου	AFM/AΦM
Hong Kong	Taxpayer Identification Number	TIN
Indonesia	Taxpayer Identification Number/Nomor Pokok Wajib Pajak	NPWP
Ireland	Personal Public Service Number	PPSN
Israel	Mispar Zehut	תוהז רפס
Italy	Codices fiscal	
Jamaica	Taxpayer Registration Number	TRN
Japan	Kojin bingo/個人番号	Mynumber
Luxembourg	Passport/Carte d'Identité	
Malaysia	Kad Pengenalan Pendaftaran Negara	NRIC
Malta	Karta ta' l-Identita'	Nru
Mexico	Número de registro federal de contribuyentes	RFC
Netherlands	Burgerservicenummer	BSN

New Zealand	Inland Revenue Department Number	IRD No
Norway	Fødselsnummer/D Nummer	
Peru	Número de registro unico de contribuyentes	RUC
Philippines	Taxpayer Identification Number	TIN
Portugal	Número de Indentificação Fiscal	NIF
Singapore	National Registration Identity Card Number	NRIC
South Africa	Taxpayers Reference Number	TRN
South Korea	Resident's Registration Number/ 주민등록번호	
Spain	Número de Identificación Fiscal	NIF
Sri Lanka	National Identity Card Number	NIC
Sweden	Personnummer/Samordningsnummer	
Switzerland	Alters und Hinterlassenenversicherung Nr	AHV-Nr/ No AVS
Taiwan	National Identification Card/國民身分證	NIC
Thailand	Personal Identification Number / เลขบัตรประชาชน	PIN
Turkey	Türkiye Cumhuriyeti Kimlik Numarası No	T.C. Kimlik
UAE	Identity Card Number/بطاقة الهوية	
USA	Social Security Number	SSN

SEARCH REGISTRIES

UK	Companies House
Australia	Australian Business Register
Belgium	Central Enterprise database
Brazil	Department of Registration and Integration (DREI)
Canada	Provincial Corporate/Business Names Registry
China	State/Provincial Administration for Industry and Commerce
Cyprus	Department of the Registrar of Companies
Denmark	Central Business Registrar
France	Register of Commerce
Germany	Handelsregister/Trade Register
Greece	General Commercial Registry
Hong Kong	Business Registration Office, IRD
Ireland	Companies Registration Office
Italy	Business Register of the Italian Chambers of Commerce
Jamaica	Office of the Registrar of Companies
Malaysia	The Registration of Business Act 1956
Mexico	Secretariat of Economy
Netherlands	Trade Register
New Zealand	Companies Office
Norway	Brønnøysund Register Centre
Philippines	Dept. of Trade and Industry Business name search
Portugal	Citizen Portal Business name search
Singapore	Accounting and Corporate Regulatory Authority
South Africa	Companies and Intellectual Property Commission
Spain	Central Mercantile Register
Sri Lanka	Dept. of Registrar of Companies
Sweden	Companies Registration Office
Switzerland	Federal Commercial Registry Office
Taiwan	Ministry of Economic Affairs
USA	State Business Entity searches

DANCE AWARDING ORGANISATIONS[1]

DAOs can be single or multi genre, and many of them operate internationally or within their sphere of influence.

The Council for Dance Drama and Musical Theatre (CDMT), an organisation based in the United Kingdom, provides quality assurance to the professional dance, drama and musical theatre industries. CDMT validates many of the world's leading awarding organisations offering performing arts qualifications. Some of these awarding organisations are also recognised by the Office of Qualifications and Examinations Regulation (Ofqual), a government department that regulates qualifications, exams and tests in England. These qualifications, exams and tests are included on the Regulated Qualifications Framework (RQF), a single framework for describing all regulated qualifications in England and vocational qualifications in Northern Ireland. The RQF is further mapped to the European Qualifications Framework (EQF), which acts as a translation device to better understand and compare qualification levels across Europe.

Council for Dance Drama and Musical Theatre (CDMT)
www.cdmt.org.uk

The DAOs below are based in the United Kingdom, some of which operate internationally:

British Association of Teachers of Dancing (BATD)
www.batd.co.uk

bbodance
www.bbo.dance

British Theatre Dance Association (BTDA)
www.btda.org.uk

Graded Qualifications Alliance (GQAL)
www.gqal.org

[1]   (CDMT, 2018)

Imperial Society of Teachers of Dancing (ISTD)
www.istd.org

International Dance Teachers' Association (IDTA)
www.idta.co.uk

National Association of Teachers of Dancing (NATD)
www.natd.org.uk

Professional Teachers of Dancing (PTD)
www.professionalteachersofdancing.co.uk

RSL (Performance Arts Awards)
www.rslawards.com

Royal Academy of Dance (RAD)
www.rad.org.uk

Russian Ballet Society (RBS)
www.russianballetsociety.co.uk

Scottish Dance Teachers' Alliance (SDTA)
www.sdta.co.uk

Spanish Dance Society (SDS)
www.spanishdancesociety.org

Trinity College London (TCL)
www.trinitycollege.co.uk

United Kingdom Alliance (UKA)
www.ukadance.co.uk

United Teachers of Dance (UTD)
www.unitedteachersofdance.co.uk

There are other international DAOs[2], some of which are:

Australia:
Australian Teachers of Dance/International (ATOD/ATODI)
www.atod.net.au

Commonwealth Society of Teachers of Dance (CSTD)
www.comdance.asn.au

---

[2] This list is not exhaustive

Ballet Australasia Ltd. (BAL)
www.dancebal.com

Canada:

Canadian Dance Teachers Association (CDTA)
www.cdtaont.com

Associated Dance Arts for Professional Teachers (ADAPT)
www.adaptsyllabus.com

Performing Arts Educators of Canada
paec.ca

Canadian DanceSport Federation
canadiandancesportfederation.ca

Shumka Dance Syllabus
www.shumka.com

China:

Beijing Dance Academy (BDA)
www.bda.edu.cn

New Zealand:

NZ Association of Modern Dance (NZAMD)
www.nzamd.co.nz

Asia Pacific Dance Association (APDA)
www.asiapacificdanceassociation.co.nz

South Africa:

South African Dance Teachers Association (SADTA)
www.sadta.co.za

Australia, Canada, Italy, South Africa and US:

Cecchetti International Societies
www.cicb.org

BIBLIOGRAPHY

ACAS. (2018, March 30). *ACAS working for everyone Home page*. Retrieved from Advisory, Conciliation and Arbitration Service Web site: http://www.acas.org.uk/index.aspx?articleid=1461

Barclay, L., Barrow, C., Barrow, P., Brooks, G., Carter, B., Catalano, F., Economy, P., Epstein, L., Gilmour, K., Hiam, A., Holden, G., Kelly, J., Laing, S., Matthews, D., Mortimer, R., Nelson, B., Peterson, S., Pettinger, R., Smith, B., Smith, C., Tiffany, P., & Tracy, J. A. (2011). *Starting & Running a Business All-in-One for Dummies* (2nd ed.). (C. Barrow, Ed.) Chichester, England: John Wiley & Sons Ltd. doi:10

Benady, D. (2018, May 30). Europe is taking the lead in data protection. *Raconteur reports, #0523*, 12.

British Franchise Association (BFA). (2018, June 6). *Welcome to the BFA*. Retrieved from British Franchise Association Web site: https://www.thebfa.org/

British Insurance Brokers Association (BIBA). (2018, June 3). *Find Insurance/ Find a Broker Service*. Retrieved from British Insurance Brokers Association Web site: https://www.biba.org.uk/find-insurance/

Cabrita, J., Perista, H., Rego, R., & Naumann, R. (2009). *Portugal: Self-employed workers*. Brussels: Observatory: EurWORK.

CDMT. (2018, June 6). *CDMT Validated Awarding Organisations*. Retrieved from Council for Dance Drama and Musicial Theatre Web site: https://cdmt.org.uk/validated-awarding-organisations

Chartered Institute of Credit Management. (2018, June 6). *Managaing Cash Flow Guides*. Retrieved from Chartered Institute of Credit Management (CICM) Web site: https://www.cicm.com/resources/cashflow-guides/

Companies Commission of Malaysia (SSM). (2018, June 6). *Registration of Business Rules 1957 (Rule 15. Business names)*. Retrieved from Companies Commission of Malaysia (SSM) Web site: http://www.ssm.com.my/acts/fscommand/pua0282y1957.htm

Companies Office of Jamaica. (2018, June 6). *Registered Business Names Act 1934*. Retrieved from Companies Office of Jamaica Web site: https://www.orcjamaica.com/uploads/RBNA%202006.pdf

Consultative Committee of Accountancy Bodies (CCAB). (2018, June 6). *Choosing an Accountant or Tax Adviser*. Retrieved from Consultative

Committee of Accountancy Bodies (CCAB) Web site: https://www.ccab.org.uk/ChoosingAccountantTaxAdviserTips.php

Dain, P. (1991). Spread the word about your school. *From Ballet to Business* (p. 6–8, Section A). London: Royal Academy of Dance.

Dyke, D. S. (2017). La vida no es la que uno vivio. *Animated.*

Enterprise Singapore. (2018, June 6). *About Enterprise Singapore.* Retrieved from Enterprise Singapore Web site: https://www.enterprisesg.gov.sg/about-us/overview

Entrepreneur Magazine. (2018, June 2). *Unique Selling Proposition (USP).* Retrieved from Entrepreneur Magazine Web site: https://www.entrepreneur.com/encyclopedia/unique-selling-proposition-usp

Flood, J. (1993). *How to run your Dance Studio like a Business* (Vols. Steps 1 – 3). Toronto, Canada: KMS Kaizen Management System.

Flood, J. (1993). Step 1 Operations and Procedures. In J. Flood, *How to run your Dance Studio like a Business.* Toronto, Canada: KMS Kaisen Management Systems.

Flood, J. (1993). Step 2 Meaningful Business Planning. In J. Flood, *How to run your Dance Studio like a Business.* Toronto, Canada: KMS Kaizen Management System.

Gibson, S. (2015). *Going Self-Employed.* London: Robinson.

Hallsworth, M. (2015 , October 22). *Reducing missed appointments.* Retrieved from Behavioural Insights Team (BIT) Web site: https://www.behaviouralinsights.co.uk/trial-results/reducing-missed-appointments/

Health and Safety Executive. (2018, June 6). *Home page.* Retrieved from Health and Safety Executive Web site: http://www.hse.gov.uk/

HM Customs and Excise. (2018, June 6). *VAT on education and vocational training (Notice 701/30).* Retrieved from Gov.UK Web site: https://www.gov.uk/Vat notice70130-education-and-vocational-training/contents

HM Government. (2018, June 1). *Contract Types and Employee Responsibilities.* Retrieved from Gov.UK Web site: https://www.gov.uk/contract-types-and-employer-responsibilities

HM Government. (2018, June 6). *Disclosure and Barring Service.* Retrieved from Gov.UK Web site: https://www.gov.uk/government/organisations/disclosure-and-barring-service

HM Government. (2018, June 6). *Expenses if you're self-employed.* Retrieved from Gov.UK Web site: https://www.gov.uk/expenses-if-youre-self-employed

HM Government. (2018, June 6). *How to classify trade marks.* Retrieved from Gov.UK Web site: https://www.gov.uk/guidance/how-to-classify-trade-marks

HM Government. (2018, June 6). *Intellectual Property Office Trade Marks.* Retrieved from Gov.UK Web site: https://www.gov.uk/topic/intellectual-property/trade-marks

HM Government. (2018, June 6). *The Charity Commission for England and Wales.* Retrieved from Gov.UK Web site: https://www.gov.uk/government/organisations/charity-commission

HM Government. (2018, June 6). *Volunteer, rights and placements.* Retrieved from Gov.UK Web site: https://www.gov.uk/volunteering

HM Government. (2018, May 17). *Welcome to GOV UK.* Retrieved from Gov. UK Web site: https://www.gov.uk

HM Government. (2018, June 6). *Working for yourself.* Retrieved August 5, 2017, from Gov.UK Web site: https://www.gov.uk/working-for-yourself/overview

Howard, S. (2016, February). Transformers. *Dance Gazette* (Issue 1/2016), pp. 22–27.

Information Commissioner's Office (ICO). (2018, June 6). *Guide to the General Data Protection Regulation (GDPR).* Retrieved from Information Commissioner's Office Web site: https://ico.org.uk/for-organisations/guide-to-the-general-data-protection-regulation-gdpr/

Kokemuller, N. (2018, June 6). *Diversification & its importance.* Retrieved from Smalbusiness.chron.com: http://smallbusiness.chron.com/diversification-its-importance-77562.html

Layups.com. (2018, June 6). *Setting Goals and Milestones with your Team.* Retrieved from Layups.com Web site: http://www.layups.com/setting-goals-and-milestones-with-your-team/

Lynn, M. (2016, January 18). *The self-employed will overtake the public sector with the "gig economy".* Retrieved from Daily Telegraph Web site: http://www.telegraph.co.uk.

Nesta. (2018, June 6). *Creative Enterprise Toolkit.* Retrieved from Nesta Web site: https://www.nesta.org.uk/toolkit/creative-enterprise-toolkit/

Nesta. (2018, June 6). *Tools and Resources.* Retrieved from Nesta Web site: https://www.nesta.org.uk/help-me-innovate/

One Dance UK. (2018, June 6). *A Guide to Careers in Dance.* Retrieved from One Dance UK Web site: http://www.onedanceuk.org/wp-content/uploads/2017/02/Careers-Guide-Digital-version.pdf

Palo Alto. (2018, June 6). *Business plan software.* Retrieved from Palo Alto Software Web site: https://www.paloalto.com/business_plan_software/sample_business_plans/dance_studio_business_plan.php

Rampton, J., (2016, August 26). *Business Plans: A Step-by-Step Guide (Article 247574).* Retrieved from Entrepreneur Magazine Web site: https://www.entrepreneur.com/article/247574

Rist, R. & Siddall, J. (2001, June). hands on … or hands off. *Dance Gazette* (Issue 2/2001), pp. 48-51.

Royal Academy of Dance. (2015). *Factsheet No 01: Buying and Selling a School.* London: Royal Academy of Dance.

Royal Academy of Dance. (2015). *Factsheet No 04: VAT and the Dance Teacher.* London: Royal Academy of Dance.

Royal Academy of Dance. (2015). *Factsheet No 08: Insurance: Professional Indemnity and Professional Product Liability.* London: Royal Academy of Dance.

Royal Academy of Dance. (2015). *Factsheet No 10: Pricing an Examination.* London: Royal Academy of Dance.

Royal Academy of Dance. (2017, March). Terms of Engagement for Self-Employed Teachers. London.

Royal Institution of Chartered Surveyors (RICS). (2018, June 6). Retrieved from Royal Institution of Chartered Surveyors.

Safe in Dance International. (2018, June 6). *Home page.* Retrieved from Safe in Dance International (SiDi) Web site: http://www.safeindance.com/

Scottish Administration. (2018, June 6). *Welcome to the Scottish Charity Regulator.* Retrieved from Office of the Scottish Charity Regulator: https://www.oscr.org.uk/

The Law Society of England and Wales. (2018, June 6). *Find a Solicitor.* Retrieved from The Law Society of England and Wales Web site: http://solicitors.lawsociety.org.uk

The Law Society of Scotland. (2018, June 3). *Find a Solicitor.* Retrieved from The Law Society of Scotland Web site: https://www.lawscot.org.uk/find-a-solicitor/

The Prince's Trust (GB). (2018, June 6). *Help-for-young-people/tools-resources/business-tools/business-plans.* Retrieved from The Princes Trust (GB) Web Site: https://www.princes-trust.org.uk//help-for-young-people/tools-resources/business-tools/business-plans

Thom, R. (1991, October). Counting the Cost of Your Business. *The Bulletin, Supplement to the Dance Gazette.*

Thom, R. (1991, June). Starting Your Own Business. *Bulletin, Supplement to the Dance Gazette.*

Thom, R. (1992–2014). *From Ballet to Business.* London, England: Royal Academy of Dance.

Thom, R. (1998, Sept). Buying and Selling a School. *Dancing Times.*

Top Achievement. (2018, June 6). *Creating Smart Goals.* Retrieved August 5, 2017, from Top Acheivement Web site: http://topachievement.com/

Wikipedia. (2018, June 6). *Crowdfunding.* Retrieved from Wikipedia Web site: https://en.wikipedia.org/wiki/Crowdfunding

Wikipedia. (2018, June 6). *Dance Education.* Retrieved from Wikipedia website: https://en.wikipedia.org/wiki/Dance_education

Wikipedia. (2018, June 6). *List of Yellow Pages.* Retrieved from Wikipedia Web site: https://en.wikipedia.org/wiki/List_of_yellow_pages

Wikipedia. (2018, June 6). *Self employment.* Retrieved from Wikipedia Web site: https://en.wikipedia.org/wiki/Self-employment

Williams, S. (2017). Financial Times Guide to Business Start Up 2017/2018. (30th ed.). followed by Harlow, United Kingdom: Pearson Education Limited.

WordStream.com. (2018, June 6). *Social Media Marketing for Businesses.* Retrieved from WordStream.com Web site: https://www.wordstream.com/social-media-marketing

REFERENCES

Useful websites

Selected websites (URLs) listed below may provide a source of information for you.

www.gov.uk is the United Kingdom public sector information website, created by the Government Digital Service to provide a single point of access to HM Government services. This publication contains public sector information sourced from www.gov.uk and licensed under the Open Government Licence v3.0.

Allowable expenses: https://www.gov.uk/expenses-if-youre-self-employed/overview

Disclosure and barring service: https://www.gov.uk/government/organisations/disclosure-and-barring-service/about

Learning about self-employment: https://www.gov.uk/topic/business-tax/self-employed/

Registering a new business: http://www.hmrc.gov.uk/gds/online/new.htm/

Registering for tax: https://www.gov.uk/log-in-file-self-assessment-tax-return/

Start-up information: https://www.gov.uk/browse/business/setting-up/

Writing a business plan: https://www.gov.uk/write-business-plan/

Trade marks: https://www.gov.uk/government/publications/how-to-classify-trade-marks/trade-mark-classification-list-of-goods-and-services

www.hse.gov.uk provides information and advice about work-related health, safety and illness from the United Kingdom independent regulator Health and Safety Executive (HSE). This publication contains public sector information published by the Health and Safety Executive and licensed under the Open Government Licence v3.0.

HSE tools
www.hse.gov.uk/guidance/index.htm
www.hse.gov.uk/opsunit/perfmeas.pdf
www.hse.gov.uk/risk/assessment.htm

ico.org.uk (Information Commissioners Office) is the United Kingdom's independent authority set up to uphold information rights in the public interest, promoting openness by public bodies and data privacy for individuals. This publication contains data protection information published by the ICO and licensed under the Open Government License v3.0.

GDPR: https://ico.org.uk/for-organisations/guide-to-the-general-data-
  protection-regulation-gdpr/

www.wikipedia.org (Wikipedia) is a free online encyclopaedia, created and edited by volunteers around the world and hosted by the Wikimedia Foundation. Selective information has been used but only where it confirms general knowledge. The re-use is licensed under the Creative Commons Attribution-Share-Alike License 3.0 (CC-BY-SA) http://creativecommons.org/licenses/by-sa/3.0/

Types of business: https://en.wikipedia.org/wiki/Types_of_business_entity

Types of employment: https://en.wikipedia.org/wiki/Employment

Types of self-employment: https://en.wikipedia.org/wiki/Self-employment

Types of TIN: https://en.wikipedia.org/wiki/Taxpayer_Identification_Number

Search registries: https://en.wikipedia.org/wiki/List_of_company_registers

Types of taxes: https://en.wikipedia.org/wiki/Consumption_tax

Types of funding: https://en.wikipedia.org/wiki/Crowdfunding

Types of insurance: https://en.wikipedia.org/wiki/Liability_insurance

Business tools

The Prince's Trust: https://www.princes-trust.org.uk//
  help-for-young-people/tools-resources/business-tools/business-plans

Palo Alto Software Ltd: www.bplans.co.uk

Sage Group plc: www.sage.com

Chartered Institute of Credit Management:
  http://www.cicm.com/resources/cashflow-guides